Mental Health

…ry:

A Guide.

Rachel Jepson

Contents

Foreword

When I was asked to contribute to this book, I couldn't decide whether to write about my own mental health, or the mental health of the music students I teach. It then struck me that the majority of the symptoms experienced are shared and part of the same echelon, albeit manifesting in a variety of ways.

The musician breed can be split into many sub groups. There are magnificent Afghan Hounds whose serenity belies a dark self-loathing. Labradors (usually drummers) thump about the place with an insatiable energy and cheeriness, which dissipates behind closed doors. French Bulldogs, the cock of the walk on stage, spend hours self-criticizing in the mirror. And don't even mention the dainty dachshunds and the adored yet fragile tightrope they trot along daily.

The musician's mask is almost absurd in its functioning, yet it sums up the human condition well. We are all a mess of contradictions. Utterly lacking in self-belief, treading water in the gargantuan surges of who-do-you-think-you-are, while being brutally compelled to share our talents in a public setting. The performance, once viewed through a more innocent lens, is now a competitive playing field. TV talent shows have taught us that music isn't about self-expression, enjoyment and magic. It's about technical prowess, looking attractive, having a sob story and being perceived as somehow better than others. Why we subject ourselves to this public flogging it is a very good question. All I know is, if it doesn't happen regularly, the black clouds gather.

I think most musicians are perfectionists. As I've got older, I've gone a bit easier on myself and tried to find the joy in what I do, above seeking the feeling of 'being the best'. In fact, it has dawned on me recently that this past pursuit is all borne from anxiety. As a female performer, with a disability, I have always felt I had double to prove. I wanted to have the most impressive voice, be the most engaging frontwoman, write the best songs. Because girls can do that, and freaks can do that too. Now I'm looking for the buzz of playing for playing's sake. I've ended up in bands where I'm not the focal point, and I love the 'backseat' role. I love the feeling of really nailing a backing vocal or piano solo, of locking in with other musicians, and of getting lost in the song.

If I was to offer any advice to fellow musicians who struggle with anxiety and depression, it would be three things. Firstly, recognize that you have worked for years and years on something, and you haven't given up. I am the queen of the abandoned project. I have a very short attention span, am very good at initiating projects and ideas, but very bad at sticking with them until fruition. I have however, spent years learning an instrument, and honing my song writing and performance skills. Celebrate your ability to stick at something and become accomplished at it. Well done.

Secondly, recognize that there's a reason you've stuck at music. You get something out of it, otherwise you wouldn't bother. I personally believe it's the best therapy available. It is self-expression, an opportunity to stimulate neural pathways that ease anxiety and a chance to touch the void of something beyond the mundane and every day. Embrace the magic.

Finally, and it's taken me about 20 years of being a touring musician to recognize this, understand that you are unique. Your voice is distinct, your musical strengths are different to the next musician's, your personality is one of a kind. This bundle of complex variables is what makes music such a beautiful thing. No two players, bands or songs are the same. So, stop competing. Stop trying to measure up and stop believing that you aren't good enough. 'Success' as a musician isn't winning a reality TV show. It's finding peace with yourself and enjoying the ride.

— CAROL HODGE
SINGER: CRASS, STEVE IGNORANT'S SLICE OF LIFE

Introduction

When I was training to be a counsellor, I had to talk very openly to people about 'my stuff'. The ethos was that you can't fully be there for others if you have issues of your own to work through. We were encouraged to share, we were encouraged to talk about things that were bothering us, question things, to keep growing and developing as a person. I had always suffered from anxiety and depression, did and still do welcome the chance to have someone listen to me, some space of my own.

As the years went by as I was training, I still found myself suffering from depression and anxiety at times. No matter what was happening in my life, how proud I was, how much I'd achieved, there was still a niggling voice saying "you're not good enough". As far as I was concerned, I was worthless, and I hated myself. This wasn't always there, but it seemed to be bubbling under the surface. I experienced a trauma a few years ago which left me in a state of absolute boundless hatred of myself. I remember being curled up on my bed, my mum stroking my hair and me, just sobbing.

It took me back to my late teens, tucked up in bed in the afternoon, Pink Moon playing on my CD player on repeat. Nick Drake, Radiohead; music providing my comfort.

During this time of intense sadness, I put on my head phones and listened to 'Born In The USA' on repeat, over and over. I watched the sun go down out of the window, slept, thought, went over things in my head. Music helped me. It always has. Without music, what would life be? Do you remember the first time you heard your favourite album? Your first gig? Which song you listened to when your first girlfriend dumped you? The albums your brother and sister used to play in their bedrooms that you'd hear echoing around the house? Music makes everything better, it always has done and it always will. If I want to dance around and be silly, I'll put on some Prince or some soft rock classics. If I'm feeling reflective, I'll whack on some Nick Drake. If I want to be inspired and energised, it would be David Bowie, Arcade Fire, Louis Barabbas. Music has saved me. I'm passionate about it.

BUT - and this is a big BUT; being involved in music has not always been easy. In fact, at times, being a singer in various guises has caused me to be downright depressed and I'm not ashamed to admit this.

When I'd finished my training as counsellor, I researched resources for musicians and depression. There wasn't a lot out there. There are a few individuals who work with musicians and mental health, and a few organizations who deal with musicians and mental health.

And then, in 2016, Help Musicians launched their survey of over 2000 musicians and mental health, and found that musicians are 70% more likely to suffer from anxiety and depression. The clouds parted, the sun came out. I basked in the glow of "It isn't just me!!!!" I read about the survey, the kinds of musicians that were taking part, the issues that were coming up. I had so many ideas of how to help! I contacted Help Musicians and met up with someone on the mental health team. We talked about ways of helping, things they had in the pipeline, so many possibilities. I started my company Counselling For Musicians and it's been full speed ahead.

I wrote an article which was published in Therapy Today, I had musicians contact me, telling me how interesting they'd found it, that they too suffered and asked if they could pass it on to musician friends. I approached a few different radio stations about an idea for a radio show I had where I interview musicians about mental health- one took me up on it and I'm so grateful - thanks Reform Radio.

I started making little differences; facilitating talk on social media and getting people thinking about the issues around mental health and music. I've spoken on conference panels about mental health and music, and provide the first and only cpd accredited course on mental health awareness in the music industry.

It's all really positive stuff and it's growing all the time. I'm meeting people frequently who want to be involved in raising awareness of this issue. Doing my radio show, I get to meet brilliant musicians who have their own experiences and I'm honoured that they share their feelings, views, inner workings with me and my listeners.

The more I approached musicians and people involved in the music industry about this book, the more it took on a life of its own. People were so willing to contribute. Understandably, some did not want their name in the book. Their experiences and what they've chose to share is just are valuable. Some of the people who contributed or were interviewed have been given a fake name at their request.

I want to point out that the vignettes throughout the book could relate to many of the issues. For example; Nina Simone could have been placed in Image, Exploitation, Creativity. Kurt Cobain could have been featured in Addiction, Creativity, Money or Age. I put them where was relevant in some way and would illustrate the points I was making.

There are a few reasons I decided to put this book together, one: I wanted to try and educate and raise awareness of mental health in the music industry- to bring to light some of the issues that musicians and music industry professionals can face and what effect these issues can have on mental health.

Two: to entertain, the parts I've written are all right, but lets face it, there are priceless stories and advice from some wonderful musicians and music industry professionals here and I've been changed by reading them. I am again completely and utterly honoured that these stories have been shared.

Three: to help and support. My hope is that others will read this and if they're feeling low, they'll take comfort from this book and realise, as I did when the survey came out in 2016 that I wasn't alone, that other musicians have also suffered with their mental health.

I am not placing blame on the music industry for every musician's anxiety and depression. I am not telling people not to become involved in the music industry. This is not a warning, it's not all doom and gloom. The music industry is wonderful in many ways. It's changing, there are opportunities for growth, innovation and creativity more than ever with the constant transformation of how music is made, performed, recorded and released.

I am, however, striving to provide support and if this book helps one person, I'll be happy.

Every client I've discussed in this book has given their permission for me to do so; they too hope this book will help.

At the end of this book, there is a directory of organisations that can help with each of the issues we talk about and more.

Thank you, and enjoy.

1. Making it

1. Making it

I host a radio show where I talk to musical guests about mental health in the music industry. Sometimes we discuss their experiences and sometimes we talk about the industry in general, how it can cause anxiety and depression or exacerbate feelings of anxiety and depression for those who already suffer.

In one show, I talked to guitarist Pete Wilson about mental health in the music industry. The term 'making it' came up, as it has in articles I've written and within a lot of client work.

"What does 'making it' mean for you?"

Pete's response was to say making a living; making a living was the pinnacle of making it. After discussing further, he admitted that his definition of making it had changed since he first started being in bands and gigging. Back then, it was landing a big record deal, touring with some big acts and being known as one of the greatest guitarists out there.

This made me think. 'Making it' is such a loaded phrase, full of expectations and dreams and dare I say it.... settling? It conjures up images of bands with their heads hung low, gigging in venues with ten people watching, but hey, one of them is a massive industry boss who's going to sign you to a £3,000,000 deal!

I put a post on social media after the show asking musicians what 'making it' meant to them. Sure enough, a lot of the responses were centred around being able to make a living and 'quit the day job'. Some of them admitted that their expectations had changed with age and experience and that if I'd asked twenty years ago, they would have said something along the lines of "hitting the big time".

And then we get into the word unsigned which again is a packed phrase. Another guest on my show, Louis Barabbas stated that he hated the word 'unsigned' that 'un' is used to describe things that are negative 'unapproved' 'unfinished' 'unwanted' etc. Louis preferred the terms 'self-published' or 'independent'. I must admit, I hadn't thought about this until Louis said it. It makes a lot of sense; there are so many stigmas around unsigned. It's used constantly in the music industry. There are radio shows dedicated to playing 'the best unsigned music'. Websites where unsigned bands can upload their music and be heard by top industry professionals. The industry is designed to make the members who aren't signed to a label feel like they should be and that this, without a shadow of doubt needs to be every musician's goal.

What does that do to a person? The constant striving to be noticed, to be the next big thing? Relying on others to validate your talents, tell you that you are good, and that you do deserve this career. It can create massive anxiety; where is the next validation coming from? Have you sent enough CD's off this week and what about that label that your friend told you about? Have you emailed them? Your locus of evaluation is always external. You need others to tell you you're good and give you the opportunities. Of course, not all musicians are striving to be heard, but within the culture of 'unsigned' and 'making it' it's difficult not to question what you're doing wrong and why you haven't been noticed.

It's a common question from people outside of the music industry: *Have you made it yet?* They may think that it's a light-hearted question as they dig you in the ribs with their fingertips. But it's not a trivial question for some. We smile *Not yet, but the band have been doing really well...* and then the need comes to justify what you've been doing; sending CD's and links off to endless labels, publishing companies, venues, and radio stations. Gigging around venues that don't pay, where promoters blame bands for not promoting the gig or 'getting their friends down' (yes, I have been there while this has happened at a club in Manchester, about another band who we were supporting who were from Sweden. I duly noted never to work with this promoter)

Being a musician is a job that you may or may not get paid for. If you are independent, you spend hours doing all of the above. And let's not forget the creative side, spending those all-important hours writing and rehearsing. You may be coming home from a full day at work, looking after your children, putting them to bed, and then starting with your second job.

Nick Drake

I love Nick Drake. I discovered his music when I was about 18. My boyfriend at the time had a cool dad who owned an even cooler album collection. I remember pulling 'Pink Moon' from the shelf and asking about it. He said I could borrow it and the rest is history. If I was ever depressed, I would put that album on repeat and let it wash over me. I still do.

Nick Drake was born in 1947 and died in 1974; he was 27.

As with Kurt Cobain and other musicians who have suffered from depression, I spoke about Nick Drake on my radio show. As I researched Nick Drake, I found myself feeling sad at discovering how he'd felt about his music, the lack of fame that he felt he'd been promised, and the obvious decline in his mental and physical health. I sympathise with those who were around him, trying to help as I read about his behaviour and the things they'd seen him say and do, especially towards the end of his life.

To go back to the start of his musical career, Nick Drake attended Cambridge University, he studied English Literature. Whilst at Cambridge, he met Robert Kirby, a music student there. Robert went on to do the string arrangements for Nick Drake's albums. Nick started playing at local bars. He enjoyed playing the guitar and singing. People commented on how tall he was, that he looked like a star. He was introduced to Joe Boyd, an American music producer who asked him for a demo. On the basis of his four-track demo, he was signed to Island records and decided to drop out of Cambridge.

He recorded the albums 'Five Leaves Left' and 'Bryter Later' which were folk albums full of strings, woodwind, a definite sound of the time, but haunting in places thanks to Drake's ethereal voice and thoughtful lyrics.

It was reported that whilst he was touring his second album, audiences were 'missing the point' and not quite getting what he was doing. The experiences of touring made him withdraw from the audience, rarely address them, tending not to look up at all. His confidence had been knocked, but it appeared to be something more than this. It was around this time that the album had been described as "an awkward mix of folk and cocktail jazz" and Bryter Layter sold around 3,000 copies, it had been a flop.

There had been reports of this time from fellow musicians and friends of Nick Drake that he had walked off stage during gigs, that he had stopped addressing audiences all together. He was diagnosed with depression and prescribed anti-depressants. The people around Nick Drake also stated that he had been taking drugs such as heroin, which wouldn't have helped his mental health.

With Pink Moon in 1972, Nick Drake had decided to go through with a stripped-down sound. It was literally him and his voice, his guitar and the odd bit of piano here and there. It's my favourite, it's the one I fell in love with. Gabrielle, Nick's sister has written about her brother and been interviewed for various documentaries over the years. She said it was around this time where things 'started to go wrong', he was apparently smoking a lot of Marijuana. People commented that he had little connection with his friends, that if he did see people, he would rarely make eye contact and would speak only if he really had to.

After the album was released, Nick Drake reportedly became more and more distant and withdrawn. He went to live with his parents which he resented but knew was necessary due to the level of depression he was experiencing. His friend Robert Kirby described a typical visit from him: "He would arrive and not talk, sit down, listen to music, have a smoke, have a drink, sleep there the night, and two or three days later he wasn't there, he'd be gone. And three months later he'd be back."

This comment stood out for me especially, writing a book about mental health in the music industry and the effects of fame or the lack thereof and your goals and expectations not being met.

In his 2006 autobiography, Joe Boyd recalled his shock at Nick Drake's comment: "[He said that] I had told him he was a genius, and others had concurred. Why wasn't he famous and rich?"

It sums it all up doesn't it? Had this been a feeling that he had been nurturing for years? Was this a recent realization?

Nick Drake took an overdose on the 25th of November 1974. He had been struggling with depression, anxiety and reportedly substance abuse. What a legacy he's left behind, but what sadness surrounding him. Nick Drake had support around, he had caring friends in the music industry and a loving family. It would seem that the people in his life did everything that they could to try and help, but that his decision had been made.

Is there a lack of understanding within the music industry? Do the industry powers that be need to be more compassionate? They are dealing with sometimes emotionally vulnerable people who are facing rejection on a daily basis. Having a thick skin is something that often comes up when talking about the musician's lifestyle. I recently read an article online from a music charity, something along the lines that it's important not to blame the music industry for mental health problems, that everyone is fighting their own battles. As I've said before on my show and in various publications, the industry may not be to blame as such. However, for anyone who is suffering from mental health issues such as depression and anxiety amongst others, this industry can inflame these issues and indeed create new mental health issues, due to the lifestyle, circumstances and other factors which we're exploring in this book.

The need to have a thick skin is something you are aware of as a musician. Whether it's the constant struggle to have your music heard, being on tour for weeks at a time away from family and friends, putting up with internet trolls, all of these matters can be harmful to a negative mental state. There is also the possibility of people berating you for being too sensitive, for not being able to let things roll off your skin. There is sometimes an expectation that to be involved in the music industry, you have to be a bit of a bastard. I have been told in the past that I'm "too nice" to be in the industry. One client I worked with was told by a booking agent that she needed to be "arrogant and unashamedly forward" if she wanted to make it.

I worked with a guitarist client who had been in a number of unsigned bands throughout his 20's and 30's, he was 46 when we encountered one another. He was becoming more and more frustrated with how things had turned out for him and at times, his frustration was turning into anger. This is a brief transcript of one session:

> *I'm just really pissed off that I've been doing this for so bloody long and nothing has come of it. I've been in some brilliant bands, but we've never 'made it' and that upsets me, it really does.*
>
> I ask him to explain "making it".
>
> *Being successful, people knowing who we are on a big scale. Making money out of it so we don't have to work anymore. The band I'm in now especially, we're brilliant. All great musicians, fantastic songs.*

I pointed out that if he works with great musicians and they have fantastic songs, that this is more than some bands who have 'made it' and an achievement to be proud of in itself. I asked him if it was possible that this would be enough for him.

> *I don't want to make out like things aren't good enough for me, like I'm putting myself and the band down, but we do deserve more than this and even though we don't talk about it a lot, I know the others feel the same. I see a band on Jools Holland and I think straight away "we're better than them" and I start to get angry about it. Why aren't we there? I'm a grown man and I still have these dreams. I don't want to let them go? Why should I?*

I could see that he was becoming angry and we explored the anger. My client has been comparing himself to other musicians, other bands, it's hard not to. Most musicians with this amount of experience will believe that they are great and just as good as more successful musicians, if not better. The 'why not me?' question is one I have a lot of experience with, and definitely a question that I've heard from other musicians over the years.

> It seems that your focus is on where your band is going to go, where you'll end up rather than enjoying where you are now and the joy of writing and performing together.

> He thinks for a moment. *I do appreciate the people I get to play with. I love playing the songs. I just wish we'd been noticed for how good we are by people in the music industry who can make things happen for us.*

And there it is, the prospect of being noticed by others, validated. The powers that be seeing you and giving you the opportunities that you only dreamed about.

Musicians are involved in music because they love it and because they need to be. They can't imagine it any other way, they must do it. It can be a compulsion for some. There are wonderful things about being a musician, some of the highest highs you can imagine. I love hearing musicians talk when they've just performed a brilliant gig. There isn't a buzz like it, experiencing it for yourself or being involved in that buzz as a third party. The issues around making it all have the potential of contributing to depression and anxiety. Expectations, the fact that you aren't where you thought you'd be by this point despite all the effort and hard work you've put into your music.

The other side of the coin is that some musicians may not be as good as they think they are or believe that they are owed something. They may have every faith in themselves and their abilities but are deluded in the level of success they think they deserve to achieve. It's important to discuss talent in this case and relate it back to the idea of making it.

I'm going to talk about something now which can be controversial, but I think it's a really great example to use as most people have been exposed to this at some point in their lives. Any TV talent show will do; there's always the same kinds of people who audition and are edited to be shown to the public. These are the people who think that they're amazing, talented and will get through to the next round. They come in, talk the talk, big themselves up, confident. Then they start to sing. Cut to the judges' faces all looking like they're stunned at how bad the person's voice is. The singer finishes, stands there looking really happy and proud and a bit nervous. When the feedback starts, they are ASTOUNDED. They just don't understand *You're joking*- they say- *I've got a brilliant voice.* Then they start to sing again and are escorted out crying. When they're shown in the area outside, they're usually with a supportive family member who is also dumbfounded.

Here is a person, of which there are many, who strongly believed that they were wonderful. The likelihood is that they were encouraged by their friends and family, such a strange phenomenon. Can people hear this? It's hard to believe that they are hearing the same thing as the audience and still telling their loved ones that they'll make it. Here is the time to stop. As the judges are famed for saying *don't quit the day job.* I went to a competitive vocal college in London when I was 21. I studied for a diploma in pop music singing, it was one of the best times of my life. I was surrounded all day every day by people wanting to play, perform, write, listen, I was immersed. Others like me!

There were always other students there who weren't as talented as others. They had little talent but had been given a place, possibly for money, possibly for pity. They knew they weren't good, but they wanted to improve their confidence and get to the point where they could stand on a stage and not feel inferior. If this had been now, I wouldn't have hesitated to ask them why. Back then, we all just presumed that these students were sick of being called quiet and had something to prove.

Then there were the students who thought they had a lot of talent but didn't. There were other musician students there, guitarists, drummers, keyboard players who all had a passion, but who weren't necessarily good.

We've all seen it. The band who turn up, they have the attitude, talk the talk and you have high hopes because of their confidence. They want to make it and they know they will. *A guy who knows someone at EMI came to our gig last week. He asked us for a demo and said he'd pass it on.*

And then they play. *Oh* you say, slightly disappointed but also interested in how they could be so confident and sure that they have the talent to make a living out of their music. Their songs are OK at a push, but there is nothing new there, nothing innovative. Their playing is competent, but the drummer is behind on the beat and doesn't look like he's enjoying himself. The singer sounds like he's trying to sound like Jim Morrison but is flat in parts. They come off stage, cocky but a couple of them of them are arguing about coming in late to one of the songs and not knowing when to finish on another.

These people who aren't at the level they think they are, they are still musicians. We mustn't forget that. However, it's unlikely (not impossible) that they will ever be at a level they think they deserve with their music.

All of them have something in common. The talent show auditionee, the tuneless singers and the delusional members of the average band. Confidence.

If we look back over the history of pop music, there are, without a doubt, artists and musicians who despite not being super brilliant at what they do, have something. They have charisma, they can work the audience. They have a lot to offer in their persona and you believe them. They might not have the best voice, but their songs speak volumes. They come onto the stage and they own it.

Where does this confidence come from? As with the talent show auditionee, this could have been nurtured from an early age. No matter what, they've had other people validate them, tell them that they're excellent. Comparing them to their favourite stars, encouraging them to get up at family events, holiday talent shows and show people what they've got.

The guitarist who dreams of being Jimi Hendrix, who listens and plays along to his favourite musicians day after day, who's never been able to get passed a certain point with his playing, but tries because he loves it. He has confidence in himself and when the others want to form a band, he's the first person they go to.

When the auditionee is told she cannot sing and she needs to *stick to the day job* she is so astounded, her whole world looks like it's come crashing down. She is sobbing, trying to plead with the judges, she just doesn't understand. There's been a complete disconnect in what she believed to be true about herself and what is the actual reality. Her self, her identity, everything is called into question. It wouldn't surprise me if, despite of the certain comfort of her previously doting family and friends, she potentially spiralled into depression because of her experience. Where does she go from here? Her dreams of making it have now become an impossibility and she's realised that just maybe, all her loved ones have been lying to her for many years.

These dreams, this alternate life that some musicians live in their heads, it can be helpful to some. It can be a drive to fuel their ambition; be the best they can be, improve and keep writing. The awareness that, although you can always achieve, "making it" might not look how you expected is really important for mental health.

I address the changes in the industry later in the book, but I find it rather exciting that the definition of making it and success are constantly changing and musicians have more control than ever before in how their careers turn out.

To end this chapter, I wanted to use a small part of musician Alexander Douglas's contribution, his full piece can be found at the end of the book. I felt that the point Alexander makes here about the rules that no one has ever been told is inspired, and so, so true.

The music industry really is a more dangerous place than people are able to get their heads around. It offers a tantalising set of prospects for creativity and self-actualisation whereas in fact the parameters are already determined and if one fits into those, the gatekeepers open the doors to a new artist who is determined to 'do what it takes to succeed.' But what is the price of success? And how does one cope when one discovers that the game one thinks one has been playing is not only not being played on a 'level playing field' but there is a set of rules that one has never been told.

SELF-CARE AND GUIDANCE

- If you are struggling to be noticed and obsess over why this hasn't happened the way you wanted or expected, stop and assess. Why are you trying to achieve a certain level of success? What happens if you get there? Are you doing this for you, or for validation from others? Or both? Do you become depressed and or anxious when you finish a great gig, and nobody tells you how great it was?

- There needs to be something in this for you; there is no point otherwise. As much as possible, try and see the music as a beautiful gift, that you have the opportunity to create and express and of course make a living out of it but that can't be your drive, or you will crash and burn at any sign of doubt, rejection or disinterest from others in your music.

- Look around at the musicians you get to play with, or if you're a solo act, look at how much power you hold when you get on stage, that this is your time to sing, play, expose your soul.

Yes, it would be fantastic if an influential person saw you and plucked you from the stage and gave you lots of money. This is unlikely but don't let that worry , upset or depress you. With changes in the industry and the way people release music, you can make a living out of your music without the backing of a label. If you have faith and can build a fan base using social media and audiences at your gigs, you have people waiting to buy your music.

- Look after yourself by turning off. This is a big theme in the book. The music industry doesn't turn off, there is always the internet and you can access that every second of the day. Try and have certain times of the day when you don't look at your phone, where you don't check Facebook or Twitter, or refrain from sending the email to the venue, that can wait until tomorrow. It really can.

- Do something for you! Whether it's writing or singing or watching Netflix, take the time to relax and again, switch off. Creatively speaking, it's a real motivator to get out and go for a walk, look around, experience life and let the inspiration come to you.

2. Everything you've dreamed of is now reality

It's becoming more and more acceptable for major artists to come out in the media and talk about their mental health struggles. This can only be a good thing - can't it?

The initial release of admitting something like that, so forbidden and frowned upon, so misunderstood, should be cathartic. Then the trolls start.

What have they got to be depressed about?

*Try working for a living, you ungrateful ***!*

I'm sick of celebrities crying about how depressed they are. I'd swap places with them any day of the week #crybabies.

There is an inherent lack of empathy, compassion and understanding with this issue. There is a presumption that because someone is famous, rich, successful, that their mental health problems disappear when they achieve their goals. Of course, we know this isn't the case. How can it be? Some of their issues may have been around achievement, but how many people do you know that are completely satisfied when they've managed to get their dream job? It's unlikely they take a deep breath and never have to worry about anything ever again.

It may be that some musicians who are at a certain level of success already have experience of depression and anxiety issues before they entered the industry, as Simon Napier Bell states in his writing. He suggests that all artists have suffered trauma and abuse and it has made them the musicians they are today. It is definitely the case that these problems can be exacerbated by the spoils of fame and success. It's no secret that there are pressures in the music industry to maintain a certain reputation, release music that is even better than what came before. Wear the right things, say the right things, have a perfect image, have an imperfect image, be a f*** up, give the fans what they want. There's pressure around giving 100% on a 90 day tour, to go on stage and not let the fatigue show. Don't let them see the sadness on your face. You've just had a phone call with someone back home and your dad is ill, but don't come home, you've got a big concert tonight!

On the other side of the spectrum, it could be that you have had no history of mental health issues at all, and then the music industry arrives and whips you off into a frenzy. You didn't expect it, but before you know it you're caught up in the lifestyle and everyone is telling you how wonderful you are, and you start to lose touch, feelings start to surface that you aren't familiar with and it's making you anxious.

This is simplifying of course. There are so many complex issues. The music industry cannot be blamed for every musician's mental health issues by any means, but I strongly believe that because of the nature and circumstances of the music industry, it can highlight any existing problems and put them under a magnifying glass.

Kurt Cobain

I was 13 when I found out Kurt Cobain had died. I remember experiencing real dread for the first time. It was confusing and scary. I was watching the news, seeing clips of sobbing fans being interviewed. Photos of the house he'd been found in were shown, the police cars surrounding it, and more photos of Kurt and Courtney Love, he and their daughter. It was my first exposure to suicide, I couldn't believe that you could kill yourself, that someone would want to do that. I remember thinking things must have been so bad for him, how sad it was that he didn't feel he had any other way. It was violent too, a bullet to the head. Since Kurt Cobain, I've had my own experiences with mental health, and worked with many suicidal clients but it doesn't get any easier to deal with for those suffering with such all-consuming depression.

Kurt Cobain was born in 1967 and died in 1994; he was 27 years old. One of many who were already in the '27 club' a group of famous and massively influential musicians who had died at the age of 27. It was no secret that Kurt Cobain suffered with drug addiction, and that he struggled with fame and overall living in limelight. With Kurt as the flagship, it seemed to me as a teenager that grunge was all about the people that didn't quite fit in.

It's been documented that before he died, his long-term partner and mother of his baby, Courtney Love staged an intervention for Kurt which friends and music industry executives who Kurt knew attended. Eventually, their efforts were successful, and he agreed to go to rehab which helped short term but alas, wasn't enough. It wasn't just substance abuse that was an issue with Kurt Cobain. He had been diagnosed with Bipolar which is a mental illness where the sufferer experiences extreme highs and periods of mania, and then crippling depression, either of which can last for hours, days, months.

In an article for The Telegraph in 2015, author Matt Haig explores our obsession with turning troubled artists into 'tortured geniuses'. This stood out to me:

"I hate this idea. The idea that creativity is the bedfellow of misery. I have also come to hate my own former silent glorifying of Cobain's death. When I was 24 I nearly took my own life, not because I'd listened to too much Nirvana, but because I was ill."

I believe that people put creativity and misery together where Kurt Cobain and other artists are concerned, the old 'Tortured soul' paradigm. Perhaps as a society, it's easier to concentrate on the music Kurt Cobain made than the mental health issues that he suffered. Kurt Cobain was diagnosed with Bipolar disorder before he was involved in the music industry but made comments during interviews that he found fame difficult to deal with and felt he couldn't protect his privacy, or the privacy of his loved ones. He was struggling with it all. He'd become an icon for many at such a young age and the poster boy for grunge, a music genre and sub culture that he was now responsible for.

The 2015 film Montage of Heck, shows us home videos of Cobain when he was a teenager, and when he's found fame. He's described by people closest to him as 'quiet' 'interesting' 'troubled'.

Within his lyrics for 'Serve the Servant', Kurt writes about child hood and it's clear that with everything that fame brought, he was dissatisfied and looking back at childhood traumas, unable to forgive and forget:

Teenage angst has paid off well
Now I'm bored and old
Self-appointed judges judge
More than they have sold

As my bones grew they did hurt
They hurt really bad
I tried hard to have a father
But instead I had a dad

The article by Matt Haig points out that Kurt was ill and that he wasn't just a miserable creative type. He had suffered pre-Nirvana, pre-fame and was struggling with inner demons that had always been present.

We discussed the idea of not being ready for fame in the chapter on Age. There are so many artists who have found difficulty with everything the music industry brings; perhaps they weren't ready, perhaps they never would have been.

Singer Chesney Hawkes was just 19 when he starred in the film 'Buddy's Song' and released the colossal hit 'The One And Only'. I thought Chesney's viewpoint on hitting the big time would be really valuable, to receive this contribution was an honour:

When you are young, you don't have the insight to know that the hype isn't real. You are at that age when you believe what everyone around is telling you, negative and positive. You believe it when people tell you that you are great and you also believe it when people tell you the opposite. You don't have the muscle yet to know the truth which is that you just have to trust yourself and not listen to anyone else's opinions or bullshit. Trying to distinguish the bullshit from the real is something that comes with experience and age. When you fully trust and believe in yourself, which at times I am still learning to do, all of the knock backs, negativity and criticism don't land quite as heavily. I have had to do a lot of soul searching and learn to love my authentic self for what I am and the gifts that I have. I have been blessed with the support of a loving family and some seriously amazing practitioners in different modalities that have given me the tools to cope with the ups and downs, the stress and anxiety of this business and life in general. It's not been an easy road and it's been bumpy for sure. I've come to realize ultimately that it comes down to me. It's my life, my choices, I'm in charge and I choose to be happy!

Robbie Williams

Robbie Williams speaks up regularly about his mental health problems and has been very open about his struggles within his music and lyrics. I admire this about Robbie Williams, everything seems to be transparent with him, he doesn't seem to be afraid to share the depression and anxiety he suffers and his battles with addiction.

Robbie has recently become the first patron for the music charity Music Support, which founded by music industry professionals and former addicts, provides many services for musicians who have substance abuse issues.

In an interview with The Sun in February this year, Robbie said that he felt fame had a big influence on his mental health-

"Depression sprints through my family. I don't know if I'd be this mentally ill without fame. I don't think it would be as gross or as powerful if it hadn't had been for fame"

Robbie rose to stardom at the age of 16 when he joined the pop band Take That as the youngest member. It's hard to imagine the effect this must have had on a young man from Stoke on Trent, propelled to this magnitude into an industry he had little experience with (his Father is a singer performing locally) and to receive praise, criticism and have access to a world that most people only dream of. He was quickly known as the joker of the band, who was extroverted and spoke out within the band and to the media, not afraid to be perceived as 'the wild one'. This is a persona which he has taken with him throughout his career. He has been described as 'Marmite'; you either love him or hate him.

Robbie Williams started using drugs and drinking excessively. By 1994, he was abusing drugs to the point where he had a near overdose. There were reportedly issues with Robbie not feeling he was being listened to within the dynamics of the band, that he wanted to experiment with hip hop and the others weren't interested. This mix of pop, indie and hip hop was to be his signature sound throughout his career.

Robbie's exploits featured in the media frequently during this time, especially when he left the band at the age of 22. He was photographed drinking and partying with celebrities and fellow musicians, George Michael and members of Oasis.

In 1996, he signed a contract for his solo career with a major label and has enjoyed massive success in the UK and other parts of the world. Robbie Williams has collaborated with colossal stars such as Kaylie Minogue and even Nicole Kidman. He has even worked with lesser known but more respected artists such as Rufus Wainwright and John Grant.

It's important to acknowledge that although a huge star, he is also in some respects the 16-year-old boy who was projected into this unknown world. I think about what I was like at 16, what boys around me were like and what effects this would have had on them. I think of young clients I've had and successful musicians I've spoken to, all with different experiences of the industry and mental health. I see the vulnerability in Robbie Williams behind the arrogant and extroverted façade, particularly since her has been so open about his mental health struggles.

"Fortunately, and unfortunately, left to my own devices, I'm inclined to sabotage everything," Robbie said. "I've got a disease that wants to kill me and it's in my head, so I have to guard against that."

"Sometimes it overwhelms me and sometimes it's a tool I need to get on stage. Sometimes I live in bliss and it's wonderful."

I recently came across the Kesha and Dr Luke story and was horrified at the way she had been treated. Lukasz Sebastian Gottwald or 'Dr Luke' worked with Kesha since she was 18. He was her producer and had reportedly been controlling and abusing her for years. The lawsuit sparked #freekesha as people wanted to see her freed from her contract with Dr Luke.

In 2014, Kesha took out a lawsuit against Dr Luke, accusing him of sexual harassment, gender violence, civil harassment, violation of California's unfair business laws, intentional infliction of emotional distress, negligent infliction of emotional distress, and negligent retention and supervision.

In one incident Kesha states that Dr. Luke, 41, made her snort a substance before boarding a plane and sexually assaulted during the flight. On another occasion, Kesha said that Dr. Luke forced her to have a drink with him and gave her what he said were 'sober pills.' Kesha claims she woke up the following afternoon, naked in Dr. Luke's bed, sore, sick, and with no memory of what had happened, so frightening.

Kesha's lawyer, Mark Geragos, told TMZ that the lawsuit is an effort for Kesha "to regain control of her music career and her personal freedom after suffering for ten years as a victim of mental manipulation, emotional abuse and an instance of sexual assault at the hands of Dr. Luke."

This situation reminds me of Brian Wilson and the controlling and abusive aspect of his relationship with Eugene Landy. However, the Kesha scenario is horrifying on so many levels, especially the drugging and sexual abuse.

There were also emails published by Kesha's legal team where her weight is discussed by Dr Luke, claiming that A-List song writers refuse to give Kesha their songs because she is gaining weight and not sticking to her diet plan. It's hard to believe that this is an issue for songwriters and that the industry is caught up in weight in this manner, especially with breakout artists such as Adele and Rag 'N' Bone Man.

In 2016, Kesha dropped the charges against Dr Luke, stating that she just wanted to get back to making music. In 2017, she released her album 'Rainbow' to widespread acclaim.

At the 2018 Grammy awards, Kesha performed her song 'praying' alongside Cyndi Lauper and other female artists as part of the #Metoo movement which was sparked by the sexual abuse scandals sweeping Hollywood. The performance was met with critical acclaim and admiration from her peers in the music industry. It was clearly an incredibly emotional moment for her and a catharsis in many respects as she was embraced by her fellow singers at the end of the song.

If we've learnt anything from Kesha's relationship with her producer was based on money, pressure, stress and control. Dr Luke had worked with other female artists such as Kelly Clarkson, who has been one of Kesha's supporters throughout this lawsuit.

Will Young

I loved watching Will Young on Pop Idol. I had been addicted to the entire series, buying Darius Danesh's album as soon as it was released. I'd found the whole thing so entertaining, I'd bought into it hook, line and sinker. All of the contestants, to me, were incredibly talented but it was Will who I'd championed. I remember watching the final and sinking to the floor screaming 'yes!!!!!!!!!' when they announced he'd won. Soon after that, there was something in the media about Will being gay, how he'd been advised to hide it but that he wasn't going to do that. We'd seen Will Young being confrontational and not accepting the injustice of his performance of 'Light My Fire' being called 'average' by Simon Cowell. And now, 16 years later, Will is still outspoken and not afraid to challenge, and I love him for that. I think it's wonderful that he's so open about his own mental health struggles and the depression, anxiety and trauma. Most recently, he pulled out of Strictly Come Dancing because of mental illness.

In an interview with The Mail On Sunday in April this year, Will talks about his experience on Pop Idol and Strictly:

"I spent decades living a life of shame and guilt. Within weeks of winning Pop Idol, I had to sit and listen to someone at my record company read out this appalling piece someone had written calling me a big-jawed gay predator, and however tough you think you are, you just go back to those awful feelings"

The awful feelings Will refers to was from being at boarding school as a child and being bullied by teachers there. He stated that seeing the adults behaving this way and experiencing the bullying meant he wasn't afraid to stand up to Simon Cowell.

That level of fame at such a young age and so suddenly must have been difficult, especially with the media writing such nasty things. It appears that Will Young has always struggled with the fame that he found early on in life, that he has never been comfortable:

"I hated being a pop star. I would never put out a record again. It makes me sick to think of being that person I knew wasn't really me. I did have some good times and did meet some very good people, but I was never comfortable, never happy. You get the record deal, the big hits, the beautiful house, but you're not right on the inside, and you either get worse and worse or you try to deal with it. You try to work out where you really want to be".

Will is now 39 and has a new role in Baz Luhrmann's stage adaptation of Strictly Ballroom. He co-hosts pod cast 'Homo Sapiens' with film maker Chris Sweeney and is very much enjoying his career.

There's no doubt that becoming a successful musician has affected the lives of so many people in different ways. Some musicians have become successful and coped extraordinarily, some have not. We've seen that there are many factors involved in these outcomes but that one thing is abundantly clear: that no matter what the situation, we need to provide as much care and support to these musicians as we would to any one else. Yes, they have experienced success and fame, but we're educated enough now to say with all confidence that this doesn't necessarily mean that a person is free from their mental health struggles, anything but.

3. Addiction

3. Addiction

For those looking to escape their addictions, the music industry is a hard place to find yourself in. The people, the lifestyle, the emotions, all conducive to wanting to escape down the rabbit hole. There are many people who would be able to resist partaking in drugs and alcohol, but those who suffer with addiction may not be able to find this peace and might not be able to say no. People who have suffered with addiction of any kind will tell you that if they're faced with the thing they're addicted to constantly, it can feel like torture.

Chris Difford, songwriter and co-founding member of the band Squeeze wrote this exclusive and candid piece:

I didn't know I had a mental illness until I found myself sitting up in bed sweating and crying with exhaustion and pain. I was further down the barrel than I had imagined. Drinking and taking drugs were an everyday event for me, it seemed normal to go to bed and pass out, to wake up shaking and confused, crying and in a state of such sadness. It seemed normal for me to lie and cheat, to ignore those close to me and hide away all the time in my imaginary sanctuary filled with more of the same each day. Friends of mine got well, they seemed like strangers, but they had something I knew I needed, I just didn't know at the time how to access it. Like all good friends they gave me time to discover sobriety for myself.

Being in the music industry at that time, the early 80's was like being on a constant binge, surrounded by like-minded drug taking and drink swilling commandos who all fought together for the same cause. We fell one by one in the trenches of the 90's. My job was to play in a band and be that guy on stage who would saunter about like a young fox, hunting for the next thrill. I had a few bob so being in the right clubs was never a problem, I was happy, or so it seemed. Gradually the curtains closed, and the darkness held me in its arms while I wilted on the vine like a forgotten grape. The illness was a perk of the job you might say. These days I avoid at all costs being around people who drink, it's not very entertaining to listen to them as they juggle nonsense before me, but then that was me, I was that person, so who am I to judge? To boundary my life is all I can do to keep sober and slightly saner than I used to be. That was then, and that person hurt so much to be the person he wanted to be, and that illness loved me more than parents every could. I was safe, so I thought, in that sadness.

The music industry has changed, and so have I. Today I never meet people who fall over themselves to give you lines of drugs or try to get you pissed, it's a thing of the past, a daily reprieve, and I'm so grateful that after 25 years on the clean step I'm slowly getting there. It's harder than ever to be on the road and in a band, it's still difficult to trust my feelings around others but somehow, I manage to navigate the good the bad and the ugly. This mental illness is never going away, it's there every day, I have to be as bright as a button to make sure it keeps away from me. How lucky I feel to have come this far in my life knowing that it's OK, it's my journey and one day at a time things keep happening. Something always happens when you let go of yourself.

I thanked Chris for his disclosure and for sharing details of his addiction. I know other musicians will relate to this. Within the writing, there's so much more than the addiction; life on the road, age and money, all issues discussed in this book in regards to music and mental health.

Chris talks of the temptation, the fact that he was simply around drugs and alcohol; it came with the lifestyle and he enjoyed partaking. I think it's really important to acknowledge that Chris says his friends got well and got the help they needed, that he recognised he needed that too and had to come to it in his own terms.

It's not uncommon in the music industry for the use of cannabis to be rife. Some people believe it makes them more creative and find it hard to do what they do without it. I have spoken to several musicians and industry professionals who smoke weed, but some have taken it to the next level. Stefan is a house DJ and producer who sent this to me, thanks Stefan.

I smoke cannabis every day. Sometimes I wake up in the morning still stoned from the night before. In some ways, I wish that I didn't have this habit. It makes me slow and unmotivated. There are things I want to do, that I need to do that I just can't when I've been smoking. But there are other times where it takes me exactly where I need to be. I create, I can maintain a wave of creativity for hours, days while I'm smoking weed. I can't always keep my promises or be where I say I'll be, but I can produce music to a standard I'm happy with and that's the sacrifice I make a lot of the time. Drugs and music over my relationships- and mental health.

I've seen cannabis affect people in different ways, depending on the level and intensity of the addiction I believe it has it's pros and cons. It can be seem as a harmless drug, one that chills you out, levels you and helps with anxiety. I have had clients who have used cannabis as a way of trying to combat their stress anxiety instead of medication prescribed by a GP. However, research has been done into the effects of cannabis on mental health both positive and negative. The Royal College of Psychiatrists maintain their research found that people who are already at risk of developing mental health problems are more likely to develop mental illness if they smoke cannabis regularly. Research has found that the levels of THC (the chemical which changes your mood when you smoke weed) in the cannabis dictates whether or not there is a likelihood that the regular user will develop psychosis and other serious mental illnesses. Let's not forget that there is a chance of developing conditions from regular cannabis use that can permanently change your brain and effect your mental health and everyone around you. Use responsibly people.

I worked with a client who had been sober for 8 years. She's a drummer and plays with a jazz band. Every year, they would go to New Orleans to a festival there and spend one week playing and partying. Here is a small excerpt from a session:

One year I just blacked out and woke up the next day with no memory of what had happened whatsoever. I was in a strange place and didn't recognise anyone in the sea of bodies.

That sounds frightening.

It was. I decided there and then that I'd stop partying and become sober.

That sounds like a difficult but brave decision, how's it been going for you?

Oh, it's a constant struggle. The friends I'd made on the road, members of the band, praying that they'd accept that I don't drink. I'd tell them I didn't want the whisky, or beer or whatever it was, and they'd respect it, but they'd bitch about it too! They'd tell me I had no willpower, that I was boring, no fun anymore. It was hard. But after a couple of years, they were OK. A couple of them even said sorry.

I've worked with clients who go on tour for months at a time, one in particular who referred to going on holiday with his "music family". He disappears from reality and allows the "whatever happens on tour stays on tour" mentality to really take hold.

He openly admitted that he drank far too much, took far too many illegal drugs and had been admitted to hospital several times for kidney and liver problems, even a suspected heart attack:

> *When I come home, I find it really hard to engage with life. My wife and kids find it difficult to adjust to me being there. It's like we're all learning from the beginning again, how to be a family. I suddenly have to pick my kids up from school, do the shopping, it's weird. I feel like I'm having withdrawals from the drugs. And my wife hates my drinking, finds me sleeping on the couch in the morning when she wants to get the kids ready for school.*
>
> And how do you feel about that, that your wife is finding you on the sofa in the morning after you've been drinking?
>
> *I feel bloody horrible. I don't want them to see that I was so drunk I couldn't make it to bed. I feel like I've failed them, but I don't know how to make it better. When I'm playing music, it's all I have to worry about, how I'm playing, whether I've missed my cue, I'm only responsible for me. I can be involved with the social stuff, you know?*
>
> It sounds like drinking and drugs is a big part of the musical lifestyle for you.
>
> *It is, sadly. I know it must sound cr**, like I'm some old rocker who doesn't know when to say no. But it's just really seductive. I love finishing a gig, being part of a really amazing f*****g band, and then celebrating, buzzing off everything until the early hours. The drugs just make the high all the higher. The drink just helps with everything. I don't feel like a failure when I'm working. I feel like I'm where I should be.*
>
> I wonder if there's a way of you still enjoying those highs, the natural buzz of music without those substances. Wouldn't that be something to aim for? Something to really be proud of?

He thinks for a minute.

> *Mmm, yeah. It would. Can't see it happening though. I like it too much.*
>
> You might enjoy it, but from what you've been telling me, it seems that you're ashamed of these addictions when you're with your family. Is there a way of having a more balanced life without the substances? It feels to me like you have two very different lives, the alcohol and drugs are representing those differences now.

There's too much tied into it. It's not simple. Sometimes, I feel like I'm at my best on drugs. That I'm the most creative I've ever been, and people are blown away by my playing. That might not be true, but it's how I feel and I don't know if I'm prepared to give that up.

Even though your life is at stake? You've had several medical emergencies including a heart attack.

*That should make me want to stop shouldn't it? When I think about what happened to me, having to go to hospital and be told if I didn't stop, I'd be putting myself at extreme risk. I just don't feel like it was me that it was happening to. If this had happened to someone I knew and loved, I'd be so frustrated and p****d off at them. I can imagine how my family must feel.*

We discussed these issues over the course of the next ten sessions. The client was at home, with his family, away from his work as a musician for around 3 months. He talked a lot about being a musician, when he first encountered drugs as part of the lifestyle, and how it had always gone hand in hand. He said when he first met his wife, she knew he had taken drugs but was under the impression he had stopped soon after they met. Clearly, he had carried on taking drugs and drinking when he was working as a musician, determined to keep the two worlds separate. He said he thought he could make it work, have these two separate lives. It was becoming more apparent as time passed that this wasn't working. He disclosed that he had tried going to rehab twice about 3 years previously, after the first heart attack. However, like the first client I mentioned in this chapter, he too felt the pressures of his fellow band members and crew and in his case, didn't feel he could resist.

As our sessions were ending, the client was starting to feel anxious. He knew that he had a few UK dates coming up touring with a well-known artist, and he recognised the familiar itch to drink and partake in whatever recreational drugs there were going around. He had made such positive progress, I wonder how he got on. I didn't see him again after our sessions. I hope that he managed to see that what he was doing didn't have to be part of the music industry experience for him, that he could be just as creative and innovative as a musician without the substances as with, if not more.

Brian Wilson

Brian Wilson was born in California in 1942. We know him best as the lead singer of the Beach Boys formed with his brothers Carl and Dennis, their cousin Mike Love and their friend Al Jardine. We also know Brian Wilson for his mental health issues, a part of his image, persona and creativity that he has discussed in recent years and that have been dramatized in the 2014 film Love & Mercy.

Whilst making the album 'Pet Sounds' in 1966, which Brian Wilson wrote, recorded and produced, he began to experience overt mental issues and had a series of nervous breakdowns. His creativity and the need to produce a masterpiece was overwhelming for him at times and he found it difficult to come to terms with his Father's constant criticism. Nothing Brian did seemed to be good enough. The other members of the band weren't sure about the songs Brian was writing, it was too far from their usual happy go lucky surfer sound. Pet Sounds is considered now to The Beach Boys best album and indeed a masterpiece.

Brian's mental health issues didn't begin with Pet Sounds, he used to suffer from agoraphobia as a teenager and wouldn't leave his room for significant periods. He felt safe in his room, so the other members of the band would come to him there and he would teach them harmonies, chords and sing them the songs he'd written. Brian's room had become a haven for him. In 1963, he wrote the song In My Room, lyrically, we can see the significance of having a sanctuary and somewhere to go when he was feeling unable to face the world.

There's a world where I can go and tell my secrets to
In my room, in my room
In this world I lock out all my worries and my fears
In my room, in my room

Do my dreaming and my scheming
Lie awake and pray
Do my crying and my sighing
Laugh at yesterday

Now it's dark and I'm alone
But I won't be afraid

In 1975, Brian became involved with Eugene Landy, a psychologist who Brian's wife had brought in to help Brian with his mental health issues. At this time, Brian was suffering severely and agreed to see Landy to avoid being sectioned into a psychiatric facility. It became clear to the other members of the band and other people close to Brian that Landy was exerting control over the man in his vulnerable state. He was telling Brian what to do creatively, professionally and financially. Landy was prescribing medication to Brian who was becoming more and more withdrawn and disconnected with reality, something that Eugene Landy was supposed to be helping with.

With help from his wife, Brian managed to end his relationship with Landy and saw another psychologist for several sessions, but who later died. Landy was unfortunately re-hired after Brian overdosed on a cocktail of drugs, alcohol and psychiatric medication. After years of control, Brian did manage to cut ties with Landy and receive help and support from professionals and those around him.

In 2004, Brian released 'Brian Wilson Presents Smile', a reworking of the Beach Boys album 'Smile'. It earned Brian Wilson his first Grammy award.

In 2015, Brian Wilson and his wife Melinda began working with charity 'Campaign to Change Direction' in raising awareness of mental health. Here is one of Brian Wilson's comments on mental health whilst being interviewed on the campaign:

"There are various forms of mental illness. One out of every five Americans suffer from mental illness. We got involved with Change Direction to help people realize what I went through and what they can get through."

The identity of some musicians is tied up with their addictions. We know incredibly talented musicians who are more famous for their substance abuse than their abilities. It's hard to break out, and there are those who are also battling with changing the focus of their persona on their music rather than their legacy of drink and drugs.

The lives of certain musicians have been well documented over the years; musicians with addictions are viewed as interesting and people are entertained when they read about them or watch documentaries. Some musicians have tried to leave their addictions behind, focus on their music and have found this difficult due to the persona that they had in the press and in the media. People didn't want to see them clean! People wanted them to be exposing themselves in public and drunkenly falling from a night club onto the street.

These artists may have become fearful of what might happen to them and their career if they do stop taking drugs and stop their wild child lifestyle. Will people still be interested in them? Will they have anything to say? Will they be relevant? I remember talking to the manager of one well known singer saying that when he had first been signed, there was pressure from the label executives to keep this singer in cocaine because 'it made him better' as a writer and performer. This, of course, wasn't the case, but it was a common perception that this singer would have been 'dull' without the drugs.

*It was easy to keep him doing what he was doing and watch the train wreck because we were all making s***loads of money out of him. Nobody wanted that to end, but we all knew what we were doing was wrong. Nobody admitted it, but it was better not to for everyone's sake. When he wasn't on the drugs, people said he was boring. His music was alright, but the fact was, it wasn't as good as when he'd had a few drinks or done some coke. What we should have done was help him, instead we helped him make a total mess of everything. I don't work with him anymore, but I hear on the grape vine that he's still on a dangerous road. As long as he's famous, nobody in this business is going to help him.*

With the money and fame of some musicians, comes the temptations of substances they previously wouldn't have been able to afford, or been tempted to take. But now, there are people telling them that they've "made it" and that they deserve to indulge. They're rich and don't have to think about blowing money on drugs and bottles of Cristal. It can be a slippery slope, one that some musicians may easily be able to resist, but that for some it can be incredibly difficult and the beginning of the end of their health, relationships and ultimately, their lives.

Janis Joplin

We know Janis Joplin as a 'party girl', free, liberal, a part of the Woodstock hippy era. She was part of the "27 club" a group of young musicians who died too soon at the age of 27. Janis was very open about using drugs and was friends with fellow musicians Jim Morrison and Jimmy Hendrix who were also famous for their drug use and who all died at the age of 27. One of her most famous quotes highlights her philosophy of how she lived her life:

"Man, I'd rather have 10 years of superhypermost than live to be 70 sitting in some goddamn chair watching television."

Janis reportedly enjoyed sexual relationships with both men and women and never labelled herself where her sexuality was concerned. Her drug use became excessive during the first part of her musical career when success and fame were presenting themselves and continued throughout. Friends around her could see that she was becoming emaciated and worried about her constantly injecting methamphetamine and heroine. They raised the money for her to go back to her parents in Texas for a natural detox and a form of rehab, this acceptance of support was short lived.

In 2015, a documentary was released by Amy Berg called Janis: Little Girl Blue. Berg used Janis's journals to put together the documentary whilst also accessing video clips of interviews and some home movies. She talks to Janis's siblings who recall seeing Janis at a massive gig and how she had been admired by the fans around her:

"When we were getting ready to leave, I remember overhearing one of my parents tell the other one, 'You know, dear, I don't think we're going to have much influence any more."

Janis projected an image of being care free and hedonistic, but she suffered from body dysmorphia, a mental health condition where sufferers focus on flaws in the appearance, flaws that are unlikely to have been noticed by others. She had been a victim of bullying for most of her school career for her appearance, including wearing short skirts and dying her hair. In an interview with The Guardian, Amy Berg makes parallels between Janis and Amy Winehouse who also suffered with body dysmorphia and addiction:

It's clear that the issue of alcohol and drugs in the music industry is not a recent phenomenon. The 1960's was probably the most prevalent era for the advocation of drugs in music. With the hippy movement and Woodstock, drinking and drugs were a way of life and represented freedom and free thinking. When we think of bands such as The Rolling Stones and The Beatles, we're aware of the level of drink and drugs that were present during their recordings, their gigs and backstage. Jimi Hendrix was found dead having choked on his own vomit. He had reportedly taken an overdose of prescription sleeping pills, it's inconclusive as to whether he intended to end his life. Jim Morrison, the lead singer of The Doors was found dead in a bathtub after a drug overdose. Alan Wilson, singer of the band Canned Heat died of a drug overdose. Brian Jones, one of the original members and founders of The Rolling Stones developed a drug problem which apparently caused him to be ousted from the band and he died in his swimming pool a few weeks later.

There's definitely a pattern here and a blatant disregard for these individuals' health and wellbeing. Would it have been possible for the powers that be in the music industry to have monitored and cared for these musicians? In Janis's case, she had friends and family who cared for her and tried to encourage her to live a healthier lifestyle. It's possible that other musicians had this support network too. Like with all addiction, it's up to the individual to acknowledge it and want to get well. Even with the help and support of industry executives, as Kurt Cobain reportedly had, nothing will work unless the musician themselves is well and truly willing. We heard from the client earlier on in this chapter, that despite major health issues and the fact that he had a family, he was still reluctant to cease drinking and taking drugs. He enjoyed it, he didn't see the urgency.

As discussed, the use of drugs, prescription or otherwise is well reported within the music industry. The media will always find the exploits of famous addicts of interest and it's the responsibility of everyone to provide support and understanding.

SELF-CARE AND GUIDANCE

- When you're a musician suffering with addiction, it's easy to say "remove yourself from the situation if you're feeling tempted to drink or partake in drug use". If you're on tour and surrounded by people who are free to drink and take drugs as they please it can be a real temptation. Even though it is difficult, being open with the people around you is the best way to ensure you can get the space you need. Explain to people what's going on, it's hard and risky as explained earlier but it's what you need to do to ensure you don't feel that pressure and help you keep on track.

- If you feel a pang of temptation and aren't sure you can resist, call someone, a sponsor, a relative, someone who knows what's going on and can support you. Put a list together of AA meetings around where you're touring, a manager may be able to help you with this.

- If you're a musician and you enjoy writing, use this as inspiration. You have the ability to pour all these feelings and emotions into your music and have a creative outlet to help yourself and others as a result.

- 'Music Support' offer a 24/7 helpline dedicated to the music industry. They specialise in addiction due to the experience of the founding trustees. They have sent musicians to rehab and liaise frequently with different services to get you care if needed. **MUSIC SUPPORT 24/7 HELPLINE- 0800 030 6789**

4. Image

4. Image

It could be argued that image within the music industry is just as important as the actual music being produced. Would Justin Bieber be as successful if he wasn't good looking? Ariane Grande's pony tail has become as iconic as her voice, and Elton John's flamboyant outfits have become as famous as his songs.

Are musicians allowed to be who they want to be? There is certainly an expectation from established artists that they look a certain way, alternatively, that they keep changing; keep the illusion that they are fresh, that their music is like nothing you've heard from them before. We often see artists re-inventing themselves, changing their hair, clothes, sound.

Not to stand out too much. Not to be too different, just a little is enough. Not to be too much like that artist but remind people of them a little because that artist sells money. Take drugs, drink, it helps with your image, people like to see that, it's part of your appeal. There is so much tied into image. I am immediately drawn to Britney Spears when I think of image and the music industry. Here is an artist who was a teenager when she was signed and moulded into the sexy young school girl seen in the 'baby one more time' video. A wholesome, but not too wholesome role model for all young girls. Beautiful, attainable and catchy pop. She started to wear more daring outfits as time went on, with each album there came a new iconic look, different hair, a red PVC jumpsuit. Then years later, we see her public break down as she shaves off all her hair.

Our image of her changed in that moment, but to her it was something much more. It seemed that she didn't care at that point, that the years of having to be a certain way and have the paparazzi follow her around everywhere had caused mental issues.

Now Britney Spears has made a comeback, but do we have more or less respect for her? She's no longer the pop princess we thought we knew , she's 'real' she's been through something we can relate to, she's made herself vulnerable but she's also been brave. I remember speaking to a few male friends at the time of Britney's breakdown. We were in a bar, and another couple of men heard what we were talking about and came over. 'Ha, yeah, Britney Spears, she's proper off her rocker now isn't she? Hard as nails, wouldn't want to meet her in a dark alley!' They were jibing one another, it seemed that a vulnerable person's mental health issues had become fodder for a leery chat in the pub, but at the same time, behind the jibing and nudging, there was a strange admiration going on for her. In their own way, they were saying 'she's alright that Britney, she's alright'.

Image is everything in this industry. It could mean the difference between selling albums and tickets to your gigs or being dropped from your label. A lot goes into an artist's image. A lot of thought and creativity goes into the look, the clothes, make-up, whether the sound matches the image, whether you see what you expect when you listen. Whether that's a good thing or not, whether a little mystery is required. It's all so carefully crafted and can lead to issues for the artist

I worked with a transgender client last year, she would prefer not to be named. This client had a lot of issues to work through on how she looked, but in particular, the way that she felt she did or didn't fit in within the music industry:

> *I look in the mirror and I don't see what most people see when they look in the mirror. I see someone who is really trying to be themselves but there are so many barriers, especially in music. I've been on stage and people have shouted stuff at me, asking me to sing Shirley Bassey, you know, making out like I'm a drag queen. I am a woman, I want to look like a woman and I'm achieving that, and I'm proud of that, but I can't seem to break out of feeling this way. I want people to hear the music. Yes, my image is a part of me, my physical identity is important, but it's not everything.*
>
> It sounds like what you're saying is that you're wanting acceptance and respect.
>
> *I do, and I also want to be heard. I'd rather be the person who makes really good music and has a great singing voice, than 'the trans singer' but I guess that's how society is going to see me, people are just getting used to this. There are some agents who approach me because they want someone trans to play at an event or something. That's happened a few times. It's great to raise the awareness of trans issues, but it would be good to be asked to do something based on music. I've always been different, I've always looked different. I've fought against people all my life and I've challenged people just by the way I choose to look. I like that*

about myself, but is this always going to be an issue when it comes to my music? Sometimes I try not to standout. I where plain clothes, do my hair and makeup, but don't wear anything to make me get noticed. I want my music to be taken seriously.

From what you're saying, it sounds like you've enjoyed challenging people with your image but that when it comes to your music, you wish it was less of an issue.

I like my image, how I look. I feel it's a work in progress, but I like it. I had photos taken a few months ago and I was so happy with them. They were like a dream come true, I'll bring them in next time. I look amazing, thanks to the photographer, but also what I wore, my makeup, the way they did my hair. I wanted one of the pictures on my album cover when I finally get around to it. But I think they're really serious too, that people will notice the images, but that the music is good and will stand up on its own. It's just so hard sometimes to look at the singers you admire and have grown up listening to and think that "I might never achieve what they've achieved because of how I look. I will never be like them.

You feel that there are a lot of barriers, but you were saying earlier that you enjoyed challenging people. I'm wondering whether the acceptance of how you look and also being trans is as significant for you as making people sit up and notice.

There are two things going on because like you say, I do want to be accepted and just be a 'normal' woman, but part of me also enjoys being a representative for trans in the music industry. I know I'm not famous or anything, but I think that I do affect people in a small and positive way. When people hear my music, yes, I want them to think 'that's really good" but I also want them to have to think about who made it, like 'this music is good, but it was made by someone trans, mmm, maybe trans people are OK'. Obviously, that's simple, but you see what I mean.

The client was going through some personal issues around being transgender, but also around music and what people would perceive when they heard it. The client enjoyed being the kind of person who challenged people, she was used to it, but she also wanted to fit in and be taken seriously. Her image meant everything to her at the time of our work together and she was just starting to establish exactly how much she valued herself and her influence on others.

Michael Jackson

Recent revelations aside, I'm writing these profiles to link mental health and the music industry, to illustrate how there are connections between these artists and the industry they chose to work in. What better way to do that than with an overview of Michael Jackson?

He is probably the most famous pop star in the world. When someone reaches that level of success and becomes an icon, it's hard to think of them as people. Imagine sitting with them and talking in the same way you would with your Gran or best friend? Yet, he was someone, he was a person issues that he had struggled with from an early age.

Everyone has an opinion on Michael Jackson, everyone knows something about him and his life. Whether it's that he had a difficult childhood, a controlling Father, massive issues with his self-image, enough to encourage him to have several surgeries. That he had these final surgeries to look like Elizabeth Taylor, and that in the end, he had an addiction to painkillers and anti-anxiety medication such as Xanax and Valium that apparently killed him.

The reason we know all of this is because he had no privacy and almost all aspects of his life were reported for public consumption. After all, when someone reaches that level of fame, isn't just expected that they hand over their rights to privacy? And this may be part of the issue with the music industry and getting everything, you wished for. That no matter what you release, what you do, everyone is watching and wanting to know what's going to happen next.

In the 1988 film 'Moonwalker' there's a scene where Michael Jackson puts on a giant bunny head and escapes from a hoard of fans and paparazzi by riding away on a motorbike, leading them on a wild chase. The soundtrack to this scene is 'Leave Me Alone', clearly showing his distain for the lack of privacy he had in his life.

It's been well documented that Michael Jackson had issues with his Father, claiming that he would whip him and his brothers if they missed a note. In one interview, he stated that his father had climbed through his bedroom window one night with a mask on to warn him of the dangers of leaving his bedroom window open.

During his childhood, his father reportedly jibed Michael constantly for having a wide nose and bad skin calling him 'ugly'. These claims were supported by his brothers who said it was 'brutal' to watch the verbal and physical abuse. His plastic surgery obsession started in the mid 80's around the time of the iconic 'Thriller' and 'Bad' albums. His nose was getting thinner, his skin lighter. By the time 'Dangerous' was released 1991, he had transformed into something that was ridiculed by the media and the public. He was criticized for being ashamed of being black, trying to be white, a bad role model for young black people. He was reportedly diagnosed with Vitiligo in the 90's and used it as a defence for the bullying he was suffering at the hands of the public. Still, people are sceptical that this was the truth, his image was so odd, the things we knew about his private life, so strange. We questioned his lifestyle, his childlike ways.

If Michael Jackson hadn't been involved in the music industry, or been famous, would he have had the issues he had? Would he have become obsessed with his image, develop body dysmorphia and become addicted to painkillers? We don't know for sure, but we can definitely agree that this was a factor in his mental health issues and his fight to maintain contentedness in his life.

Are musicians allowed to be themselves in the music industry? This is such a controversial debate. Largely, there is pressure to conform to the needs of the audience, and of the music industry executives who are under pressure to deliver a certain look, a certain sound in the artist they were expecting. Some musicians have been 'allowed' to be themselves and they've become famous for it. Some have been told to look a certain way as it will be more accessible.

The Spice Girls are the biggest selling girl group of all time. They were icons of the 90's and the forefront of the 'Girl Power' movement. This was dismissed as some as a clever marketing ploy, but many girls around that time, me included, felt empowered by them. The image they portrayed was that friends were all that mattered, and you could relax, chill out and just be yourselves. Each and every one of The Spice Girls had a very distinctive image. This was apparently carefully crafted at the time of their release to the world as being aimed at young girls. The nicknames 'Posh', 'Sporty', 'Baby', 'Scary' and 'Ginger' were invented by Top Of The Pops magazine and adopted as naturally as their own given names. They all wore clothes matching their image, posed in pictures perfectly acting the part. Baby would smile sweetly with her feet turned inward, wearing a baby doll dress and bunches. Scary would leer at the camera and be larger than life, wearing her hair 'wildly' around her, in camouflage pants and a crop top. Ginger would have bright red hair, stick her tongue out or do a 'peace' sign, wearing skimpy clothes. Sporty would have her hair scraped back, wearing tracksuit bottoms and a crop top, perhaps in a 'hard' stance and posh would look very serious, wearing a tight dress and have her sleek black hair cut into a neat bun. It was genius, their image, the marketing around them. We look at those pictures now and remember exactly who everyone was, their persona. As they matured, their image still stuck but their clothes and hair became a little slicker, less 'rough around the edges'.

Since her time in The Spice Girls, Melanie Chisholm confessed that she suffered from depression and eating disorders and exercised obsessively. She disclosed that couldn't look herself in the mirror at the height of The Spice Girls fame.

Karen Carpenter

Karen Carpenter was born in 1950 and died in 1983, she was 32 years old. Karen famously suffered from anorexia which was eventually the cause of her death. She seemed to be enjoying a surge of good health and positivity before she died after suffering from the condition for around 20 years. Anorexia can put strain on the heart due to the constant weight loss and weight gain and inconsistency in diet and nutrients ingested.

Karen reportedly suffered from anorexia since she was in high school, so it was present before she became involved in the music industry. She formed The Carpenters with her brother Richard after being a part of various musical groups. They were signed to a major label in 1969 and have become one of the most successful pop acts of all time. Karen was famous for her beautiful Contralto vocals, allowing her to sing comfortably in a lower register with stunning effect.

It has been Karen Carpenter's issues around anorexia that has been responsible for raising awareness of the condition, at a time where it was relatively unknown.

In 1973, The duos success was at it's peak, and Karen Carpenter saw a photograph of herself performing at a concert. The photo made her look slightly larger than usual and this apparently sent her into a tail spin. She hired a personal trainer who encouraged a high carb diet, causing her to build muscle. Karen didn't like the way she looked and felt she was even heavier. She fired the personal trainer and went on a diet she had created, whilst also doing exercise. Whilst doing this diet, she weighed

7 stone 12 pounds, which was dangerously underweight for a person of her height. Not only did Karen continue the diet, but she announced she wanted to lose 5 more pounds to be her ideal weight.

Here is an example of a musician who already suffered from a mental health issue becoming worse whilst being involved in the industry. Seeing the photograph of herself triggered a dangerous string of events which led to Karen being hospitalized and eventually to her death. Karen seemed to have received support from those around her, but there was a lack of awareness about the issue of anorexia, but additionally around the effects of fame and the criticism surrounding the music industry.

This is something we discuss in the chapter on Gender, but is there more pressure on women to look a certain way? Does this mean they sell more albums? I believe the term 'sex sells' is true to an extent, but does this term relate more to a certain demographic? I don't think I care if Lady Gaga looks great in her new video, but is this a subliminal thing? And equally, do I want Tom Waits to look like Sh** on his new album cover? Like he's been through the mill? Like he's got something to say? Of course I do!

The image of women in the music industry is expected to be more polished, there's no room for a bit of stubble or some underarm hair. In a similar theme to that of Karen Carpenter, American singer Kelly Clarkson told CNN in October 2017:

I was miserable like inside and out for 4 years of my life. But nobody cared, because aesthetically you make sense.

She went on to say: *Just to clear something up, I wasn't miserable because I had to be thin, I said I was miserable, and as a result, I became thin.*

When a journalist asked: *Did Kelly Clarkson eat all of her backing singers?* Kelly replied:

I'm awesome! It doesn't bother me, it's a free world. Say what you will. I've just never cared what people think. It's more if I'm happy and I'm confident and feeling good, that's always been my thing. And more so now, since having a family. I don't seek out any other acceptance.

Boy George

George Alan O'Dowd has maintained a career within the music industry for over 30 years. He is currently one of the judges 'The Voice Australia' along with Kelly Rowland and Joe Jonas. Recently, he has announced that his original band, Culture Club have reformed and will be on tour this year.

It's not easy to ignore Boy George, and it would appear that's exactly what he wanted from an early age. He has a beautiful voice, but it's his image that has stood him apart from other acts and has made him an icon. His image sparked controversy and there were questions over his sexuality, but being bisexual was something that he was open about. He was a young white man wearing make up, dread locks, trench coats and bowler hats. He confused people. In his late 50's he still makes a statement with his appearance.

He stated in an interview with Chrissy Iley in 2015:

"Jimmy Somerville [from The Communards] was the first gay pop star and I think that counts as something quite big. My thing was not about being gay, Jimmy's was."

In the mid 80's, Boy George was in the midst of a battle with drug addiction and was arrested for possession of Cannabis. He was also an alcoholic and has been clean since 2008, he states that he still goes to AA meetings. He was also arrested for assault on a male escort, something that he feels extremely guilty about and has openly cried about during interviews. He said:

"As a recovering addict you can't blame anyone for the choices you make."

Band members were confused by Boy George's choice to continuously take drugs and drink. Jon Moss stated in an interview in 2014:

"The unhappiest moment was when George decided taking heroin was a better career move than making another album."

In 1986, Rolling Stone magazine wrote a piece about Boy George's appearance at a charity concert in June that same year. Michael Goldberg wrote that he had become emaciated and 'was desperately trying to do something about his makeup'. He also reported that Boy George was 'doing as much as two grams of heroin a day'. His iconic look had changed dramatically, and he had cut his hair and wore a cap. He also wore clothes with offensive slogans, but one that said, 'Heroin Free Zone'. The audience responded to his solo set by throwing bottles and cans at him.

"Before leaving the stage, George bid the crowd a sarcastic goodbye from 'your favourite drug addict'."

Like with Robbie Williams and other musicians, Boy George had found success and fame at a young age and had become addicted to the money, the adoration and the access to drugs.

He has been clean and sober for years and is apparently also 'gluten free'.

Boy George admitted recently on the show Loose Women, that he had suffered from panic attacks on a regular basis and had admitted himself to hospital several times thinking he was dying. He told the panellists that his condition was 'really hard to diagnose' and that it could be caused by coffee, stress, and other factors.

"Eventually somebody just said to me, 'You need to learn how to breathe, change your diet, maybe try yoga...' just calming down.

It wasn't chest pains ... just panic. It's not logical. Sometimes there's no symptoms, you're just like, 'What's wrong with me?' You just lose it."

There's a lot in image, we've seen how it can relate to mental health; simply by being a tool allowing a musician to express themselves as with Boy George and The Spice Girls. It can also be a clever marketing tool connecting an audience to an artist and stabilising, in some cases, a life long love affair. Musicians can change their image on a regular basis if they feel they need to. Each album that is released can lead to a new image. It's a way of re-invention, either with or without the music that accompanies it.

Image can also relate to mental health in the music industry in terms of how we see the musician. As we discussed earlier, Britney's Spears breakdown and head shaving is the image that comes to mind, but it suddenly gave her respect from people who wouldn't usual be a fan of Britney Spears. She had mental health issues at the time, sure, but she was now 'a loose cannon' and many more people had become voyeurs to her breakdown.

The audience also identify with Kelly Clarkson, someone who's weight fluctuates. When we see an image of her, we immediately judge and assess 'is she in a thin phase, or a fat phase?'. However, Clarkson herself has clearly stated that she doesn't care what anyone thinks. The image of a musician is important to us.

When we think purely of images of mental health in music, a few come to mind. The bloody image Richie Edwards from The Manic Street Preachers carving 'FOR REAL' into his arm in 1991 after then NME journalist Steve Lamacq asking him if he was 'for real'. The images of Amy Winehouse drastically losing weight and looking emaciated with her trademark beehive and tattoos. Sinead O'Connor's incredibly brave video posting in which she sobs into the camera lens about being alone and suicidal. We see what people want us to see when it comes to mental health in music. Richie Edwards talked a lot about depression, self-harm and eating disorders. Amy Winehouse was actually a shy and private person who seemingly had become lost and clearly didn't want to be seen how she was seen. Sinead O'Connor was helpless. She needed help, she knew it, she is reportedly getting the help that she now needs.

Image is so powerful in the music industry that it is s a tool that is used to sell, to draw people in, to shock and to exploit. The mental health of musicians should be the priority when it comes to image; nobody should be made to look a certain way, nobody should be told that if they gain weight, lose weight or anything else, that people will no longer be interested in their music. Certain individuals need to gain more of an understanding of what these pressures on image can do to a person and that the musical output needs to be the main focus.

5. Changes in the industry

While the idea of being spotted by a major record label and being catapulted to fame may be still there for some musicians, it's starting to become an ever fading dream. People are starting to become more accepting of the fact that the industry is changing, but for some, it's with a great reluctance.

I have to admit that I, myself have had difficulties when it comes to accepting the changes. I now embrace them and see the positives, but after close to 2 decades of being in a certain mind set, it took a string of events for me to let go of the old ideals.

From the age of 17 until around 2 years ago, I was very much of the mind that if you work hard, keep playing gigs, keep putting stuff out there, keep emailing and sending then someone will notice and give you all that you deserve.

I do still think that if you keep at something, good things will happen, but how do you measure 'good'? I believe hard work pays. I believe that if you're talented and have the goods, people will notice and buy your music and come to your gigs. However, what has changed is the way you go about achieving the success you want, and alongside the earlier chapter of Making It, accepting that whilst you may not be signed to a million pound record deal, you can release your music and MAKE A LIVING OUT OF IT!

Yes! You too can record your own music, promote it, perform it and sell it yourself to minimal cost. It's called a cottage industry, grass roots, getting down to basics. Some would argue it strips music right down to what it should be; all about the music, the artist and what they have to offer the audience and that they simply want to make a living.

It's easy to be seduced by the many companies on social media claiming to help you make a 6-figure salary through your music if you buy their package of online workshops. They're embracing the change and you could argue- exploiting it? I don't see it like that. I see that they are sharing their knowledge, and yes, they are making money out this, but some of the knowledge and tips do genuinely work, I speak from experience.

It took my a long while, but with the help of other musicians and indeed doing my research and work in mental health and the music industry, I can see that there are other ways to do this. Ways in which you are still in control, where you can feel fulfilled and full of pride that people are interested and wanting to buy your music directly from you!

I'm no longer wondering what the labels are interested in, whether they'd like my new material, because I can play and sell straight to the fans, and doesn't that mean a lot? I've been asked to speak at several conferences about music and mental health and it's really encouraging to see that there are a growing number of services for people wanting advice and guidance in the independent side of the industry.

But with change comes letting go and this can be frightening. It can cause anxiety and in this instance, it could lead to depression. In a way, when I realized that I could do things a different way, I felt like I'd wasted a lot of time and energy and that my mental health had suffered as a result. A void had opened up too. What would I now do other than record, send my CD's off and email people in order to get a response, make them listen to my music, make them respond! I was admitting I'd made a mistake. I found it hard to adjust to say the least.

I spoke to a Manchester based band called Quids, made up of Rhona on vocals, Jon on guitar and Sam on Keys. They shared a similar experience to mine, now they seem to be thriving in their own way and loving their freedom:

> Rhona- *From being a child, I never wanted to be in music. My dad is a musician and I saw how down he was sometimes, that he couldn't support us financially in the way he'd like to. But as I grew up, I started singing and playing and writing stuff and I knew I was like him, and that music was something I wanted to work on, make a living out of.*
>
> Jon - *I didn't get into playing the guitar until I was about 18, but I picked it up really quickly. It was only when a friend told me they thought I was good that I started to think about being in a band. I'm really happy they did tell me that, I wouldn't be sitting here with these fine people today!*

Rhona- *You big softy Jon.*

Jon- *It's true, it's awesome.*

Sam- *I always played the piano, mainly classical stuff. My parents were really into classical music. Strict is the wrong word, but they definitely took me and my brother's musicality really seriously. It was important to them that we all practiced, took our exams. I know a lot of children would have hated that and rebelled, but we really liked it. I'm grateful to them now for encouraging us so much. I met Rhona at a party and she and Jon were already working together, writing and rehearsing weren't you?*

Rhona- *Yeah, we'd known each other for about a year when you and I bumped into each other. It all worked really well right away. We all got on, we all had similar tastes in music for the most part. We just meshed right away.*

Jon- *Part of the reason we all gelled was our aspirations. The fact that Rhona and Sam were both quite driven, and I wasn't at first. In a way, it's them who have inspired me to care more and think of the future. They bring out this side of me that wasn't there before, I like that but it also made me care about what people thought damn it!*

Rhona- *It's good though isn't it Jon? Caring? (they all laugh) I think that Sam and I really wanted to get somewhere with out stuff, we knew it was great and we could see the future, you know, what bands we sound like, who we could play with, what venues we could play at...*

Sam- *And what we wanted out of it. I think 'get somewhere' kind of sums it up, but at first we weren't sure what 'somewhere'. I always imagined playing piano for orchestras but had really enjoyed the freelance work I'd had. We love our music, our songs. There was one rehearsal imparticular where we were all like 'yeah, this is something we're going to work on and put a lot of energy into and see where it goes'.*

Jon- *I started imagining a big, you know, music label executive coming to our gig and telling us afterwards that he was going to sign us to a multi million pound record deal! It was really clear to me. 'If you do this, this and this, then this will happen' there was no room for failure as far as I was concerned. I didn't realize I thought like this until a while after and we started doing the independent stuff.*

Rhona- *I was similar really, I think that there is an old model of the music industry that no longer exists for most musicians, and so you just had to carve something out for yourselves, otherwise you would go mad. Where was our music going to go? Where was that 'somewhere'? We sat around one time and started talking about it didn't we. Jon was actually pretty down weren't you?*

Jon- *I was, yeah. I was angry more than anything. I was pacing around a bit you know, 'why hasn't this person emailed back, why hasn't that show asked us to be on? We're just as good as that band.*

Sam- *I think we all felt it, but for me and Rhona it was a bit different because we'd had a couple of conversations previously about independent music and how we could maybe release our own stuff and what that would mean for us and what we could do, who to contact, who to use. It was quite exciting when we said that to Jon for the first time.*

Jon- *I remember feeling excited but also really sceptical. I wanted this to be a thing that worked, but my heart was sinking a bit. It was weird, but it was a bit like pity. I was thinking 'you think that, but I'll carry on trying to sort out a way we can really get noticed' I was a bit bitter, I was like that for a little bit to be honest.*

Rhona- *Yeah, I remember that, no matter what we said, you'd act like you were humouring us. I think the turning point was when we recorded the album. We'd all put our own money into it, totally self funded. We asked a friend to do the art work, we started selling it at gigs. And then we discovered the streaming sites, and places like CD Baby who would put all of your stuff on I-tunes etc and also sell the physical cd's if people wanted them.*

Sam- *Then there was the matter of promotion wasn't there? Because I bloody hated Twitter and all that! I really couldn't be doing with it, but I knew we had to.*

Jon- *I wasn't keen, but we did start tweeting, putting stuff out on social media. We got some help from a friend who worked in PR, some advice rather. They really helped and we made some changes to how we worded stuff. It was really great. I started to think 'mmm, this is actually alright' Obviously, we weren't making the mad bucks, but we were doing something, we weren't just waiting for someone to come along.*

Rhona- *We were in control.*

Jon- *Right! And we started to get fans. We had been hunting them down on social media! We had been chipping away. It made so much sense that this was our space to help ourselves for free. Twitter and Tumblr had become my office. I work from home anyway, so it was easy for me to work and get on doing a bit of music promotion.*

Sam- *Just to give you some numbers, when we started this in 2014, we'd sold roughly 300 albums, now it's 2018 and 4 years and 2 more albums later, we've sold around 10,000 albums. We charge different prices depending on what format you buy it, but with merch and other stuff, we've made, well, you can figure it out. And that's in 4 years.*

Rhona- *We mean this will all of our hearts, but if we can do it, you definitely can.*

Jon- *It took some adjustment, mentally, for me anyway. But if someone told me 5 years ago 'you're going to be in this band, making music you love, with people you love, and making money, have complete control, I wouldn't have believed it. That music exec has drifted further from my mind.*

Sam- *Who needs that m*********r?!*

Jon- *Exactly! Who needs that a*****e?!*

Rhona- *What Jon said is true, if we can do it, anyone can. And don't get us wrong, it takes a lot of hard work and a lot of faith, but if you're already doing it, if you're already making good music, all the other stuff just comes as second nature after a while.*

Sam- *Yeah, it might not be for everyone but it worked for us. And this book is about mental health right? So I just think that to help as many musicians as possible, as many artists wanting to make a living and get their music out there, make the transition over to thinking about releasing your stuff independently.*

Jon- *It sounds a little cheesy, but you're in control of your dream if you do that. It's you that gets to decide and it's you who has the chance to build up a fanbase. Good luck to anyone trying this!*

I couldn't have put any of that better myself. And it is important to note that this band were working as a team, they were all putting equal amounts of time and energy and money into promoting the band. If that is not the case with you or your band, things might become difficult and might create issues in itself. It must be something you've all agreed on, to prevent feelings of resentment and inequality.

In December 2017, The Independent featured an article called 'How Independent Artists Have Changed The Music Industry'. In it, Daniel Khalili-Tari talks about independent artists such as Stormzy 'are emerging as the new profiteers, and more importantly, the owners of their own culture'

He discussed independent black artist re claiming their culture, their music and not having to have the backing of a major label. With the emergence of successful independent artists comes the potential collaborations with bigger artists on those major labels, hence promoting the independent artist further and giving them opportunities they wouldn't have ordinarily gained.

The ever increasing interest in British rap has led to major labels to make concessions in order to get an artist on board. Universal Music Group created subsidiary label 54 in London, so that Stefflon Don would sign. The deal allowed Stefflon to sign her label to Universal granting her full artistic control over her own music.

The article states that many independent musicians have openly stated that they would never sign to a major label and 'not interested in getting commercial support'.

Such an interesting and welcome diversion from the issue of 'Making it' and what that means.

Will these changes in the industry mean that the major labels are no longer as important? I think they already do.

Therefore, it's up to musicians to question they way they can go about dealing with their music. They do have focus and control over their music. They aren't waiting for someone t come along and do this for them. They can have an independent career. Their self worth is no longer tied up in others to an extent. They have the ability to decide, the intelligence is handed back to them to do with that they see fit.

The changes in the industry aren't always going to be a good thing for musicians. The way we access and buy music now means that at the touch of a button we can have an album on our phone. People absorb the music differently. They are generally less tolerant of songs that they don't particularly like. Younger listeners will listen to songs rather than whole albums. When I was younger, this was not the case and I try and instil the same ethos into my children. I want them to listen to an album, there are songs that you don't always like right away, that grow on you in time, that may become your favourites. I feel anyone who isn't listening to a whole album and allowing these songs to grown on them are missing out on so much, and not giving themselves the opportunity to enjoy new music. That may be a bold statement, but I'm not the first person who's commented on the fact that people just aren't listening to albums anymore.

I spoke to Becci, a student studying music in Manchester. She is in a band with two of her friends and they have just recorded an album.

We were really conscious while we were recording our album that people don't listen to albums as much anymore. We didn't want it to affect what we were doing, our sound or the songs we were putting down, but it inevitably did. Each song was written with that in mind I think, and by the end we were all a little but apprehensive about the process. It's not that we weren't proud, but we did listen back thinking 'would we have written the song like that and put that melody in etc if we hadn't wanted each song to be 'catchy'? It did warp everything we did. We also had a friend who's worked with bands before and was in the industry, and he was advising us to make sure that 'each song stood out' which is really hard!

In the end, I think what we produced was something that could have been better, purely because of how we wrote it and what we had in mind. Now I'm like 'does it matter if each song stands out? Does it matter if people don't listen to the whole album? If people like that exist, we don't want them to bother listening at all!' you can become quite defensive about your music as you can hear! I still listen to whole albums. I still listen to CD's! I put a CD on, lie on the sofa and listen to the whole thing, even the ones I wasn't too keen on when I first heard, I really like now. And that's because I've bothered to listen, I've let myself hear it and not been like 'no, lets skip that one'. It bothers me that people do that. That we live in a world where artist have made something and nobody endures it, nobody sits with it and lets themselves be bored. It's got to be 'now! Now! Now!' There's a great song on The Suburbs by Arcade Fire called 'We Used To Wait' and it's about that very thing, but there's great lyrics where he's saying people are in a concert and singing 'we want to heat the chorus again!' like they're so impatient that they just can't listen to a song in it's entirety. I'm ranting, I know. Albums are a funny thing, I feel we need to keep them alive and keep making them, I'd be so sad if people stopped making albums. What's the alternative? That every few weeks, bands will release a new song for people to hear? It's just not right. I don't like the sound of that world.

And thanks to Becci for that, it seems like a common theme when you look into how people are consuming music. I agree with many of the points that Becci made, is that what will become of the industry? That instead of the latest Radiohead album, you'll end up with a couple of songs every so often? I feel that we need the whole product, the musicians surely needs that process to be more intense. Recording a couple of songs at a time can be great, but it's that more long-term effort and project that contributes to the making of great musicians, that collaboration of everyone's efforts into 12 songs.

SELF-CARE AND GUIDANCE

There are a lot of companies, especially when you go on your social media accounts, who claim to be able to help you make Hundreds of thousands of pounds from your music. Some of these may be legitimate, do your research, ask others to help you do research if you can. Ask questions of other musicians you know, try and gauge the lay of the land.

Like Quids, assess what you want from the future, how you can realistically get there, what streaming sites etc you would like to use and research cost.

Do still do all the things you enjoyed within music, performing, sending your stuff out there, if that's something you like to do. It's not completely futile to hand flyers out at gigs, sell your merchandise, talk to people who may know people. There's a fine line between networking and chasing something that's not within your reach at this time.

6. Age

When I was 21, a music producer said to me: *If you don't make it by the time you're 24, you might as well give up.* I carried this with me for years. Once I surpassed the age of 24, I questioned that statement and looked around me at my peers and the musicians I respected who were all older than 24. That couldn't be right could it? Of course, it wasn't. It's surprising how common this kind of misconception is and how harmful it can be to mental health. Not only are we in a highly competitive industry but throw age in there too and it's just another reason to be anxious and feel bad about yourself.

The producer who said that to me was very heavily based in pop. He had produced the big pop acts of the time such Spice Girls and S Club 7 etc. These acts were marketed largely on their appearance, beautiful and youthful. Yes, this was brilliant pop music and 'the whole package' concept worked, but it strikes me now that this unnecessary perception has very little basis in our reality.

In my introduction, I touched upon the changing industry and how the opportunity for innovation and diversity is stronger than ever. There's room in music for everyone, no matter how old you are.

I worked with a client earlier this year who was really struggling with the ageing process. He was a guitarist in a well know band, the average age of the band was 30. We explored feelings of becoming older and how he felt on the issue. Firstly, he said that he had always thought that he would look in the mirror and see himself. When we talked about this further, the client disclosed that he had been feeling lately like he was ageing physically, and that he still felt the same as he did a decade ago. He told me that in music, people notice when you don't look the same anymore and they 'aren't interested' once you get older. This immediately concerned me, due to my own experiences, alarm bells sounded. I wondered where this had come from, this view on age in music.

It turned out that the client had been in a meeting eight years previously with a record industry executive and he had said to the band: *You have to make your mark in the next three years, otherwise people will lose interest, and you'll be nothing.* It all made sense. Another ancient view on the industry and assumptions on what people may or may not be interested in.

This is so harmful to the mental health of musicians, what does that say about their worth? About what they have to offer? Putting a timeline on talent and telling someone that they're basically worthless to everyone once they start getting older, potentially causing both depression and anxiety is not acceptable. These views seem to be purely based on image, nothing to do with what the musician has to offer musically. Athletes have a limited time in their fields, once they get to a certain age, they may not be able to physically offer what they used to when they were younger. Their abilities are not the same. However, when it comes to music, surely a musical artist will only have more to offer the older they become? They have simply experienced more, been through some stuff, you know? things have gone wrong for them, things have gone right. We want to hear this music!

The issue of age doesn't just effect musicians within the industry. I spoke with a producer recently who was having reservations about working on a certain project. At that point he said he was told 'if you don't want to do this, someone younger and fresher will'. This seems like a threat 'remember who you are and how you got here. You're old now and there are always someone who will do what you won't'. The phrase 'younger and fresher' go nicely together, but in terms of the work a producer does, does age have to equal lack of 'freshness' that you'd bring to a project? Surely, it's more to do with your experience and knowledge of that genre?:

I just couldn't believe that I was being chastised for this... The feelings I had towards the project had nothing to do with my age or theirs, I just didn't like the music. I turned it down firmly and will do the same thing again if I don't want to work with someone. I'm not being bullied into doing something because my career is being threatened.

There is pressure from all sides when it comes to age and the music industry. Are you able to do this anymore? Do you have your finger on the pulse? Are you up to date with the latest acts, the latest trends? What the young people are interested in? And do you have to be young to be able to do all of that? Will a 50-year-old man be able to gauge what the youth of today are listening to and find another Kendrick Lamar?

In the chapter on 'Making it', age was mentioned. It directly correlated with the client's thoughts, feelings and emotions on his dreams and whether he should have achieved more at the age he had reached. I don't think that it's the client's age that is the issue here, rather the pressure he has put on himself over time and this has accumulated in feelings of failure as he has grown and developed.

I worked with a client who was an artist manager. The client didn't always bring music and his job into the sessions, he'd been suffering from grief and needed to explore this. However, there was a session that I want to use here, the client has given permission for me to do so:

> *There've been a handful of times that I can remember where I've had to turn someone down or break someone's heart, crush their spirits and it's really stayed with me.*
>
> Crush their spirits? There's a powerful phrase, and you're giving yourself a lot of responsibility in that scenario.
>
> *Well, yeah. It's me doing it, nobody else. They didn't come to me feeling bad about themselves, I made that happen.*
>
> And how did you crush their spirits and make them feel bad about themselves?
>
> *I told them that they were too old. I told them that if they had come to me ten years ago, I would have been able to work with them. It was f**** horrible.*

The client sits in silence for a few minutes.

> *I got into this game because I loved music and I wanted to make some money, have some glamour, meet like-minded people. We're talking twenty-five years ago. This I'm telling you about happened about eight or nine years ago. It was a bloke in his late thirties and he was really good. One of my biggest regrets. He sounded like Adam Levine and his songs were brilliant, he made me emotional quite a rare thing when you're listening to music all the time.*
>
> It sounds like all the ingredients were there, but that age was a barrier that you couldn't see past.
>
> *Yeah, and saying this now, I feel really stupid. What an idiot. You know why I did it? Why I turned him down? I had this bloke in my head that I used to work with. He was my boss, thought he knew a lot, I looked up to him. He told me never to sign anyone over thirty, because they were more difficult to work with.*

> *He said younger musicians were easier to manipulate in a manner of speaking. It always stayed with me. And so, I went against my better judgement and I told him what I did. I could see by his face that he was gutted and didn't understand. I really hope that it didn't put him off and affect him too much and that he's still out there doing it.*

This session re-affirmed my own feelings on the subject at the time and it brought back all those emotions about age that I had nurtured due to what I myself had been told. I was angry at my client for telling the musician that he was too old, I wanted to find the musician and talk to him, ask him how those words had affected him. I didn't of course, but maybe he will read this one day and be comforted?

Imagine hearing that; believing in yourself, knowing that you were talented, having dreams and goals and then being told you're too old to be managed. Not many would have the capability of shrugging that off and move on unscathed.

On the flipside of that, I spoke to someone at a music conference who works at a small, independent label. She told me that they love hiring older bands and acts as they feel the material is enriched and they have a story to tell.

There's definitely an issue with age and image and how we perceive the ageing process. In our society, it's seen as a bad thing, something to be halted, cheated, not accepted. We're so used to having images presented to us on a daily basis, we can't even filter them anymore. Pop ups on our social media, adverts on tv and billboards when we're on the bus. Some people are breaking through that, massive beauty corporations hiring older film stars to advertise their products, people like Laura Dern and Julianna Moore. It's positive but is it enough?

Stevie Nicks

Like Brian Wilson, Stevie Nicks also had issues with addiction and sought help. She was in and out of rehab for 10 years in the 1980's after battles with drugs and alcohol. Whilst being interviewed for Women's Hour in 2013, Stevie Nicks disclosed that her psychiatrist during this time had been more like a 'groupie' than a psychiatrist and that she believed he just wanted his 'showbiz fix' and wasn't genuinely interested in helping her. During interview with Rolling Stone in 2017, she had this to say:

"How about my early-forties self? That's when I walked out of Betty Ford after beating coke. I spent two months doing so well. But all my business managers and everyone were urging me to go to this guy who was supposedly the darling of the psychiatrists. That was the guy who put me on Klonopin. This is the man who made me go from 123 pounds to almost 170 pounds at five feet two. He stole eight years of my life."

Stevie Nicks has also been very open on her struggles with depression and the reasons for her turning to alcohol and drugs in the first place. As we discuss in the book, it isn't just down to the lifestyle of a musician, although that has a large part to play. Some musicians may have an underlying depression which started before they found success. In 1979, Stevie reportedly aborted a child whom she had with singer Don Henley. She said in an interview that she would have named the child 'Sara'. One of her most famous songs 'Sara' is said to have been named after the baby she lost.

In an interview with Vanity Fair in 2013, Stevie Nicks cited the popular tv show 'Game of Thrones' as helping her get through a bout of depression after the death of her mother. She said that not only did the show distract her when she didn't want to leave the house, but that she was inspired to write poetry on each of the characters and said, "I'd love to write some music for the show".

It's clear that at 68, Stevie Nicks is still going as strong as ever, she battled with addiction and she has experienced depression and anxiety. In relation to her work ethic, it's a worry that she feels she must never stop. I hope she's taking time to look after herself and listen to her needs. However, Stevie Nicks has been so successful for such a long time that I'm sure she's aware of what makes her tick and what she needs to do to feel like herself.

"I work very, very hard. I have a piece of typewritten paper here that says, "You keep going and you don't stop." You do your vocal lesson. I have a lot of friends from high school and college who want to hang out when I play in their city. I have to rest for my show. It breaks my heart, but what comes first? Don't endanger my show. That's been my mantra my whole life: Don't endanger my show."

Clearly, there are still older musicians in the industry and thriving. We still see The Rolling Stones selling tickets by the millions, Madonna, James Taylor, there's still a massive market there. But would these artists have been signed today at their current age? Would they have been signed in any era at the age they are now? The obsession that we have with age has seeped into our judgement on which music we listen to and we may have become prejudiced. It has probably always been like this.

I've always been open minded and eclectic with my musical choices but is this the same for everyone?

When I talk to friends about this point, Seasick Steve is always brought up. He was 'old' when he was signed, he has a successful career and is still going strong.

'Older' artists like Madonna are frequently criticized for their choices on clothes, make up, behaviour. I can only imagine what effects aging has had on an artist who is so huge and iconic and perhaps feels a pressure to be relevant. At a time where she should be creating and being thankful for what she has and who she is, she seems to be striving to fit in and be relevant.

There is a lot tied up in age, as we've seen from earlier in the chapter. There are values, self-worth, failure, achievement, pride, shame, image and acceptance that things are not how they used to be.

It seems that although people aren't ready to reject you 'just because' you're getting older; it's always an issue I'll be wary of within the industry and I would love it if new and fresh older acts were signed and promoted and sold millions and records- that would be something.

Of course, it works the other way too. Much younger people are becoming involved in the music industry and it's is happening more and more thanks to talent shows and the constant encouragement that 'you can be famous if you just....'. There have always been young pop stars, musicians, artists. It's always a worry to see a young artist hitting fame at such a rate. It's no secret that there has been a history of young people in music that have not coped well.

Britney Spears was just 11 years old when she starred in The Mickey Mouse Club and was only a couple of years later signed to a major label. When 'Baby One More Time' was released in 1998 Britney was only 17. When most teenagers are hanging out with friends, going to school, deciding what college to go to, she was in the recording studio, doing endless promotion and going on massive tours. In 2013, 'E!' made a documentary about Britney Spears. She was filmed preparing for a 2-year Las Vegas run which started in December 2013. She stated: *I felt alienated from the public. But as time passed, the paparazzi lightened up and went away, after I wouldn't come out of the house for 2 years. I'm not saying it's good to be a bi**h but a lot of times in this industry, it's better to speak up and say what's on your mind, which I have a problem with.*

In an interview with Cosmopolitan last year, she talked about her 2007 break down. *I think I had to give myself more breaks in my career and take responsibility for my mental health.*

She went on to say: *My life was controlled by too many people that doesn't really let you be yourself. In that situation, when you are not in control, you become less excited and there's less passion when it comes to music. I wrote back then, that I was lost and didn't know what to do with myself. I was trying to please everyone around me because that's who I am deep down inside. There are moments when I look back and think 'what the hell was I thinking?*

It must have been so difficult for Britney Spears to have any sense of self that wasn't given to her by anyone else or by her public persona. Who was she? As she stated, she spent so much time wanting to please everyone, she forgot about herself and her own needs.

Justin Bieber

Justin Bieber is one of the biggest pop stars on the planet. He's achieved a lot since he started out and has also spoken up about his mental health issues. Justin was born in Canada in 1994 and was interested in performing at an early age. His mother started posting YouTube clips of him singing and within 2 years, he'd signed a massive record deal with Usher at 12 years old. He's had multi-platinum albums, won Grammy awards and broke all sorts of records for album sales and videos watched. He is reportedly worth around $265,000,000 from his music, modelling and endorsements.

In 2015, The Guardian spoke to Justin Bieber who said that achieving fame as a child was "the toughest thing in the world."

"Like Kylie Jenner. Look at her world. She's been living on tv since she was a kid. Every time she's looking around, she sees a camera and that's affecting how she's thinking, how she's perceiving people and why she has to do certain things... Situations that happen taint your mind, especially in this industry. Especially for girls."

He said he was close to calling it a day in the music industry and that he would tell himself that he wasn't good enough, that people hated him. He stopped a show in Norway after just one song and walked away. He claimed the audience in the first front rows weren't listening to him. "I don't always handle things the right way, but I'm human and I'm working on getting better at responding, not reacting"

There were times earlier in the year when Justin Bieber threatened to quite the music industry for good. This threat was short lived, but the intentions were there. His feelings towards the music industry and everything that goes along with the fame and attention was clearly enough to encourage him to make that statement. He has been open about his periods of depression and anxiety and this can only be a positive thing for other young stars looking to 'make it', and to anyone who thinks that fame means happiness.

These young artists are being told how special they are all the time by the people around them, and this is being validated by the hundreds of thousands of fans they have gained along the way. Heaven forbid something happens where they realize they're not as special as they've been told. Their entire self-worth is tied up in their music, their image, what people tell them about themselves. In the chapters on 'Making It' and 'Creativity' we talk about validation from others and what receiving or not receiving that validation feels like, and what it does to a person's mental health.

During an interview with the Evening Standard in 2013, The Sugababes talked about the effects of fame when they had started out at the age of 13 in 1998. The group split apart after 3 years, one of the members was replaced and another member of the trio left after 3 more years. The Sugababes reunited in 2003 and relaunched their career. Keisha said of the band: *We've now built a fresh, adult relationship.*

Siobhan Donaghy, one of the original members stated: *The adults around us maybe forgot we were young and our happiness was important. We were teenagers. We weren't even old enough to drink! They saw us as interchangeable- it was all about the band, not the individuals, and that's not good for your self-esteem.*

Another original member of The Sugababes, Mutya Buena said that she would never allow her daughter to follow in her footsteps and become involved in the music industry. *Make sure you have the right support and backing. Take your time and remember talent never dies.*

Actors Will Smith and Jada Pinkett Smith's daughter Willow was just 10 years old when she released her first single. Of course, she is from a 'showbiz' family, but does that make it any easier? Did she know what she was letting herself in for? In some ways, having a foundation in the entertainment industry could have helped for those reasons, however, this young child is still opening herself up to negativity, criticism, bullying and so much more a lot earlier in life than her peers.

I've talked about Michael Jackson in another chapter, he is a pop star well known for finding fame as a child. Taunted by his own father and brothers over the way he looked. Where was the understanding and support for Michael Jackson? The people who were supposed to help and protect him were the perpetrators of his negative self-image and self-esteem.

In an article called 'child performer' from Psychology Today in 2011, Wanda Behrens-Horrell investigates why some children who become stars at an early age come through it unscathed. She argues that it's down to the motivation of the child and parent as well as the child's age, length of time in the spotlight, level of commitment, work environment and financial gains. She mainly talks about child actors, but I think the theory behind what Wanda is saying definitely relates here:-

Is it possible to be a child actor and develop normally? Only if the parents do what is in the best interest of the child's development and well-being.

I wonder what the best interests of a child musician would be? If it's both the child and the parent who want to pursue a career in music with the view to finding success and eventually fame, then there definitely needs to be a support network in place. It would be beneficial for any child who is about to enter a career of any kind to have the opportunity to discuss their feelings around it, i.e. what happens if they don't succeed or things don't turn out the way they had been told they might. Again, like with other issues discussed in the book, we've discovered that some of the factors that contribute to mental health in the music industry are around validation and being told that you are as good as you thought, and here is the money, record deal and success to prove it. These are all valuable lessons to learn at any age, but the industry must be mindful of the health and wellbeing of younger people starting a musical career and the affects that the music industry can have on potentially vulnerable young people. What all these factors come down to is inherent lack of awareness and safeguarding for not just young musicians, but for all people involved in the music industry.

SELF-CARE AND GUIDANCE

- If you are a young person considering a career in music, talk to someone about your expectations and have as clear an idea as possible on what you want to do and the path you want to take.

- If you are a parent with a child interested in pursuing a career in the music industry, make sure you discuss their motives for doing this and what their expectations are. As a parent, it is your responsibility to manage the expectations whilst still being encouraging and supportive, not an easy thing to do.

- If this young musician has the talent and need guidance, seek out someone who can help, a teacher or tutor who works with that instrument. Talk to them about possible career paths.

- Just be there for the young artist, whether you're a parent, manager, whatever your role is in their life. They may be entering a time of great wonder and excitement, but also massive uncertainty and confusion. Allow them to talk, get their feelings out.

7. Creativity

The very nature of being a musician is to be creative. As a singer songwriter, you might be pouring your heart and soul into your music and performing to audiences, exposing your fears, your loves, your inner most feelings. As a working session musician, you might be playing the music you've been given and may have been hired for your unique experience and ability to take something and change it, put your own stamp on it, have creative control. You might be a producer, working on an artist's sound by using a certain sample or knowing which drum kit to use for the exact result you want.

The term 'tortured artist' is banded about a lot and in some cases, it's true. An artist in any medium can find themselves struggling to get their feelings out, needing an outlet, but also being able to express themselves in a way that other people cannot. Artists have a way, they can show people how they're feeling and what they're going through. The idea is that a musician has been so traumatized by events due to the engagement in their surroundings and relationships, that they are tortured by their emotions and choose to wallow in them. This is the nature of some artists but is this a reflection on mental health? Do all musicians suffer from mental health issues? Do all creative people suffer from mental health issues?

By having a creative outlet for ourselves as musicians, this can be incredibly therapeutic, but does it also mean that we are protective of our material? We want it to be heard and are so involved that any mistakes or misinterpretation can create negative thoughts that can be harmful? Does Eric Clapton feel like sobbing every time he performs 'Tears from Heaven' or Ben Folds when he performs 'Brick' for the thousandth time in twenty years? Are musicians literally torturing themselves when they put their darkest thoughts and emotions in a song and are destined to perform it or hear it on the stereo for years to come?

I was fortunate enough to see the wonderful Hak Baker live in Manchester this year. He was gracious enough to answer some questions I had for him on this book. He was very open about crying to the audience during and after the song 'Tom' about his friend who had died whilst Hak was in prison.

With certain songs such as 'Tom', they obviously affect you singing them on stage night after night and reliving certain memories. How does singing emotionally significant songs affect you?

I ain't scared to be me so I'm ready to show them kind of feelings on stage. If I cry, I cry, it's cool. No biggy.

I also asked Hak if having a creative outlet helped him when he was feeling low, and if he found that he was more productive when he was depressed. He answered 'yes' to both. I also asked if it was important for him to get validation from people around his songs and whether he ever worried what people thought of his music;

I have, but the people that feel it, they get it. that's it, I don't care really.

There is an interesting argument that the music industry wants to keep certain artists depressed and emotional, the artists who are known for their melancholy. Isn't that what their audience want after all? Simon Napier Bell's comments in the final chapter perpetrate this.

Are musicians pre-disposed to depression purely because they are creative?

From my own experience, putting my feelings, emotions and experiences into a song is really cathartic. If I'm going through a particularly rough patch mentally, I'll write and sing and maybe it will make the album, maybe not. The process of the writing and the singing is the important factor, and I'm lucky to have that as a tool to self-care, I find it therapeutic. When I've been in a good place and have heard that song, yes, I've become sad, but I can handle it in small doses. Artists who are well known for certain songs sing those songs over and over and try to be OK the next day, even if they're in a vulnerable state to begin with.

Bruce Springsteen

Bruce Springsteen is one of my favourite musicians. I love his voice, his sound, the way that even in his 60's, even as a millionaire, he convinces me and many others that he's still a working-class guy trying to support himself and his family. In his album 'Wrecking Ball' he sings about the depression, American's losing their jobs and homes, the state of the nation. He sings it with grit, we believe him.

I've read a lot about Bruce Springsteen, most recently his autobiography, Born to Run, where he accounts his journey into and through the music industry up to present day, talking about each of the albums he's recorded and the events around those times. However, it was only in a radio interview a couple of years ago that I heard him talk about depression. He's always been open about it, I'm not sure how this could have escaped me. Suddenly, as if it was even at all possible, Bruce Springsteen just became even cooler.

6 years ago, in an interview with The New Yorker, he talks openly about his struggle with depression and what he believes to be some of the causes. That innate creativity and 'self-loathing' are the main factors towards mental health issues:

"My issues weren't as obvious as drugs, they were quieter – just as problematic, but quieter. With all artists, because of the undertow of history and self-loathing, there is a tremendous push toward self-obliteration that occurs onstage ... You are free of yourself for those hours; all the voices in your head are gone. Just gone. There's no room for them. There's one voice, the voice you're speaking in. I'm 30 years in analysis! You think, 'I don't like anything I'm seeing, I don't like anything I'm doing', but I need to change myself, I need to transform myself.

I do not know a single artist who does not run on that fuel, if you are extremely pleased with yourself, nobody would be f*****g doing it! Brando would not have acted. Dylan wouldn't have written Like a Rolling Stone. James Brown wouldn't have gone 'Unh!' He wouldn't have searched that one-beat down that was so hard. That's a motivation, that element of 'I need to remake myself, my town, my audience' – the desire for renewal."

And there we have it, the boss himself explaining the power of the mental health issues that have been deeply ingrained throughout time in many other musicians. Like Simon Napier Bell, Springsteen is saying here that the motivation for great artists, including himself, is the 'desire for renewal'. Behind that, I'm seeing a desire to change, to make things better 'If I just do this, maybe I won't hate myself as much as I do'.

His absolute undivided attention and energy has been well documented when it comes to creating. The people around Bruce Springsteen have commented on how much of a perfectionist he is, that 'he would write 5 songs to get 1 song' as his long-time saxophonist and friend Clarence Clements would say. In a recent documentary 'The Defiant Ones' Bruce Springsteen is interviewed about his relationship with producer and engineer Jimmy Iovine. Iovine comments on his first recording session with Bruce on 'Born to Run'. He comments on the amount of takes they did to get the right drum sound, that it took days and that he was ready to walk out until the studio manager had a stern word with him, a word that changed his life and his future.

I absolutely love this quote from Springsteen which for me, epitomizes his creative ethos:

"You pull something that doesn't exist out of the air. It doesn't exist... on any given night when you're standing there in front of you audience. Nothing exists in that space until you go 1,2,3,4 VOOM. You and the audience together manifest an entire world. An entire set of values. An entire way of thinking about your life and the world around you. An entire set of possibilities. That can never be taken away."

He has also commented on the writing process, where his inspiration comes from:

"There were a lot of teachers. I didn't think I had a great talent, I thought I'd be someone who had to work harder than the next guy. And when I was a kid I did work harder, I'd be in my room 8 hours, 6 hours [playing guitar]. At the dance I'd be the guy watching the guitar player all night long.

I felt like It was something I was going to have work at very hard to do well. And the rest is a certain amount of psychology that comes with what kind of person are you.

Are you a watcher? Are you somebody who jumps in and is active right away or do you watch? Do you stand back and observe? My nature was always to stand back and watch the way things interrelate. What was going on around me. I was too frightened to join, I didn't know how to join in. Observation is a large part of my psychology.

And that has a lot to do with people who go on to write or take their own thoughts and formulate them in to something. Result of a variety of dysfunctions that you've managed to channel into some positive and creative rather than destructive. It came out of that need to sort myself out... So, part of it was natural, and part of it I worked really hard at."

Many of the people who have contributed to this book have commented on creativity. Some have stated that working in music has helped them express their feelings, given them an outlet. Some have even said that being depressed has encouraged them write some of their best work.

An interview (turned counselling session!) with Will really explains creativity beautifully. Thanks Will:

You say you've come to the session today with feelings of anxiety and depression, how long have you been feeling like this?

Erm, I'd say I've always had some form of depression, I just don't think I knew what it was ten years ago. I would go through times where I just wouldn't get out of bed for days and nobody knew what was going on. I think my mum just thought I was being a moody teenager.

And how were you in all of that? What was going on for you when you wouldn't get out of bed?

I just felt like I was worthless, there was no point in getting out of bed. There was nothing to get up for and everyone would be better off without me.

Did you ever have thoughts of ending your life?

Yes. Doesn't everyone at some point though? More 'what would it be like if I wasn't here? Would anyone miss me?' kind of thing. I didn't feel I had a purpose and I was doing OK in school but not massively, I was getting C's and stuff and I didn't feel I was getting a lot of support.

So this was ten years ago and you were in school? From what you're saying, there wasn't a lot of support around you from family or at school.

Exactly. It was all down to me and that's when I discovered – drum roll...... hip hop. Will laughs.

It literally changed my life. I honestly don't think I'd be here today if I hadn't found it.

That's a powerful statement

It is, but it's true. It got me out of bed, it got me listening to things, understanding things, hearing other people's stories. Nothing had ever done that before. I listened to music, I'd obviously heard hip hop before, but this was different.

What was different?

Eminem. I thought he was sick, he's lost it a bit now but he was...there was nobody else like him. He was incredible. The stuff he talked about, the things that came out of his mouth, out of his mind. He was so honest. And he felt like me, he'd been depressed, and he didn't mind talking about it. He made me want to write, he made me want to rap and talk about how I felt. Talk about my friends, my family, stuff that had happened around where I lived. I started to listen to others, really listen.

So, you could finally express how you felt.

*Yes! I could, and I was s***! I had zero talent and I just was so bad. But I kept at it, I was passionate. I decided that it was something I wanted to do and even if I didn't make any money, I loved writing and rapping in my bedroom, it was the best thing, the best thing. I was rapping about all sorts, but it was all coming out. Every teacher who'd ever p**** me off, every friend, girls I liked, it was all there. Don't get me wrong, there were still days where I'd want to stay in bed, and I would, but I'd do it listening to The Roots and I'd feel a little better.*

It sounds like a real comfort to you. And I'm wondering around the feelings of depression you talked about earlier and whether music still has this effect?

More than ever. I can pick up my laptop and program some music and write and it does make me feel better. The only problem is that I'm always asking myself 'is this any good?' but I'm sure other people do that too. Especially when they're not feeling right either. I'll give you an example. Last week, my girlfriend told me that she'd been for a drink with this guy from work who she knows I don't like. When I asked her about it, she said they're just friends and that it was his birthday and nobody else could go and she felt bad. Now, that sounds fishy to me. I didn't say that though. I went and wrote a really good tune and I got it out. Didn't feel any better, but at least it stopped me asking her about it when she got home and sounding like a jealous fool.

Creativity sounds like a really important tool for you to explore your feelings.

Yeah. I wouldn't live without being able to do that. I don't understand how people can't do that. I don't get it. If everyone wrote a song or even a poem or anything artistic after they'd had an argument, the world would be a better place.

Will's interview shows the effects of creativity in the therapeutic environment beautifully. I'm sure there are people reading this now and resonating with Will and how he feels.

If you're not a writer, if you're a musician who just loves to play, just playing and escaping into that music is so positive for mental health.

On the flipside of this, there is something which I mentioned earlier. Does being creative mean you're pre-disposed to mental health issues? Kay Redfield Jamison has researched artistic temperament and manic depression and found that there are definite correlations between creativity and mental health. Within her work, she was mainly investigating Bipolar, a mental health issue which we are hearing more and more about, thanks to well-known celebrities talking about it openly.

It's a common belief that artists are 'tortured'. Some believe that this makes the artist better, that in some way the key to the creative output is their mood. This was illustrated in Simon Napier Bell's contribution where he was talking about whatever trauma or abuse a musician has suffered, they will pour that into their music.

I relate strongly to the aspects of creativity and music that mean we do pour our heart and soul into our work, then send it out to be heard by others. Before this happens, it's still pure in a way. It's your baby, you love it, nurture it, think it's wonderful. You can't wait to hear what people think but are a little anxious too. What if people don't like it? What if nobody listens? What does that mean for the musician who has spent all that creative energy to receive very little in return in terms of validation?

Elliott Smith

Elliott Smith is one of the world's best loved singer songwriters. His songs have featured in films, tv shows and he has inspired many successful musicians. If there's any truth to Simon Napier Bells' theory that all good artists have suffered abuse or trauma as a child, Elliott Smith may just be it. He reportedly had a bad relationship with his stepfather, Charlie Welch. The name 'Charlie' features in some of Elliott Smith's songs and he writes about him in the song "Some Song". He claims that his stepfather sexually abused him, he went to live with his biological father when he was 14 years old.

Elliott Smith started playing in bands when he was in high school, and he also started using drugs and drinking around this time. He struggled with drugs and alcohol throughout his life and according to friends, suffered from depression. In 1994, he began his solo career and was signed to various independent labels. When his song 'Miss Misery' was featured on the Good Will Hunting soundtrack, his fame began to grow, and the song was nominated for an Academy Award in 1998.

Towards the end of his life, Elliott Smith started exhibiting paranoia, mistrust and early signs of psychosis. He told friends he believed a van was following him around and asked people to drop him off a distance away from the recording studio. He believed that DreamWorks, his record label at the time were following him and that someone had broken into his house and stolen song recordings from him.

Elliott Smith was found in LA at the age of 34 with stab wounds to his chest. There was no evidence either way of whether the wounds were caused by himself or someone else, but the consensus was that it was a suicide and there were no suspicious circumstances.

Whilst hosting the radio show, I have had the pleasure of meeting and talking to some wonderful musicians and hearing unique perspectives on a range of issues affecting musicians and mental health. Some said that the creative process was necessary, wonderful, but exhausting. From personal experience, it's very difficult to separate the creative process from the expectations you have of that work. It has certainly led me into periods of anxiety and depression and fed into my feelings of being 'not good enough' and rejected as a result. We touched on this during the chapter on Making It, that need for validation. Some musicians aren't responsible for the creative element, they are there to play music others have written. For the ones who have created it, there is a need to have that music, the hard work, received and praised.

Singer, songwriter and Vocal Coach Alena Herel said this as part of her contribution. It really sums up that very fine line between having the talent to create but also knowing that it will 'presented' to others which leads to a myriad of consequences.

Most of the creatives that I know who suffer with depression seem to be quite confident and outgoing, but in their own space they withdraw and struggle with life. (These are usually the people who compose and create from scratch as opposed to those who read music and perform what's in front of them.)

The fear of sharing your heart can cause immense anxiety. If you're a creator, sharing your work with others can throw up so many different feelings and questions such as - will people like it? Will they like me? Will they think it's good? Will they think I'm good? If they don't like it, is that because I'm rubbish and not good enough? In particular if you write and perform your own original music/material, there's a lot of emotions and questions attached to your work. If you're not strong mentally, it can wreak havoc with your self-belief and how you view yourself, which can then impact on your state of mind and emotional well-being

Ian Curtis

Ian Curtis committed suicide at the age of 23. He had been suffering with seizures and blackouts through epilepsy which diagnosed in 21 and which were getting more and more frequent. By all accounts, Ian Curtis also had a very complicated love life which was also becoming overwhelming and hard to manage. He had married Deborah Woodruff when they were 16 and had a daughter who was born when he was 19. Ian Curtis was reportedly having an affair with Annik Honore, a journalist and music promotor. Deborah was aware of the affair, but the couple remained married until she found him after he had committed suicide in their home.

Ian Curtis was known on stage for his erratic and unique dancing. Some have commented that he may be unconsciously re-enacting his fits on stage, perhaps it was a kind of catharsis and therapy for him. Curtis was suffering from depression previous to his diagnosis of epilepsy, but there was no doubt that he found the diagnosis difficult to process and it massively contributed to his suicidal ideation.

Ian's lyrics reflected his depression. His music allowed him to express much darker ideas and insights than we were used to in music until that point. Love Will Tear Us Apart beautifully illustrates Ian Curtis's feelings around the time of his relationship issues with Deborah and the darkness and loneliness he experienced.

You cry out in your sleep,
All my failings exposed.
And there's a taste in my mouth,
As desperation takes hold.
Just that something so good
Just can't function no more.

Ian was interested in philosophy and literature and won many awards at school for his abilities in these subjects. His interest in music was tied up in the sounds of artists such as David Bowie and Jim Morrison, known for their poetic lyrics. According to one source, Ian, from a working-class family, had very little money in his teens and used to steal records from music shops around Manchester, giving him access to unknown pleasures.

I talked about Ian Curtis during one of my radio shows where I played some of his music and gave a brief overview of his struggles. It made me curious as to what the rest of the band felt about him. There were various statements saying that people had asked Ian if he was alright and he just ignored them or just gave a brief 'yes'.

Whilst researching Ian Curtis, I came across this article which Joy Division and New Order bassist, Peter Hook wrote. For me, it sums up the feeling of helplessness he and the rest of the band must have felt when they realized that they couldn't help him.

Ian's illness was getting worse and we didn't help him, through ignorance really. But also, Ian was his own worst enemy – he never wanted to upset you, so he'd tell you what you wanted to hear. So, we never knew what he was suffering or thinking.

He made two unsuccessful attempts at suicide. First, when he was really drunk, he self-harmed – chopped himself up with a kitchen knife, which I think was an Iggy Pop moment out of sheer frustration. Then he took an overdose. Tony Wilson, the boss of our label, Factory Records, brought him to rehearsal – straight from the hospital, I think. We'd ask: "Is everything all right, mate?" and he'd reply: "Yeah, fine, let's carry on." As an adult and a father now, I feel guiltier than I ever did then. If that had been my son, I'd have gone round there and head-butted Rob Gretton, our manager, and taken him home. But there were doctors, consultants, psychiatrists, and not one of them was able to sort it out. Unbelievable.

We talk about how managers and other industry professionals deal with artists who have mental health issues within this book. This snippet from Peter Hook does give us an insight into the way the industry does treat mental illness and the choices that are made when someone is in need of help and support.

SELF-CARE AND GUIDANCE

- When you are feeling down, depressed or hopeless, remember that nobody has written the songs you have written, has your voice or talent. You are unique. Each new song or piece of music you write is completely yours and doesn't have to be heard by anyone else. If it is, then great, but try not to make the validation of others your goal.

- When you are suffering, do sit down and write music if you can. Being able to pour your emotions into a song is such a gift and not everyone has that.

- If singing or playing the same emotive songs frequently is taking its toll on your mental health, do take a break for however long you can or need. Clearly, you're not in the right space to be doing this right now and there's no shame in taking a bit of time for yourself so that you can come back refreshed and ready to do this.

- If you're under pressure to produce work but feel you are having an artistic block, try and seek out other musicians where you can talk and bounce ideas of one another. You could also try taking a break, going somewhere, taking a trip, walking around your local town or city to rouse some emotions and become inspired.

8. Life on tour

8. Life on tour

I've worked with clients who are professional musicians and their way of life means being on tour for months at a time. As mentioned in the chapter on alcohol and addiction, life on tour can be strenuous for some. I have friends who are musicians and feel that they're away from home far too much but love being a musician and can't turn work down. Being torn between family and work is something that many people must face, whether they're in the music industry or not, but life on tour is a different beast.

Are you seeing a theme here? All these issues tie in to one another. Life on tour can involve drugs and alcohol, depending on the band you are or the band you're touring with, there can be questions of "making it". Life on tour also brings the question of money and some musicians who are touring with bands as session musicians feel they aren't being paid enough and that their working conditions and accommodation could be better.

I've talked to musicians who are young and struggling to tour on a small budget. They may have pooled their money together to hire a van and are touring the country doing badly paid gigs to make a name for themselves. Not able to afford accommodation, they end up sleeping in their van at night to save on costs. I know some people will be reading this and thinking "well isn't that their choice? They could get a job in an office and wouldn't have to worry about it". Of course, this may be the case, but this is a life they have chosen, and like anyone, they deserve autonomy, respect and support.

I'd like to focus on this for a little bit; the battle that musicians come up against whilst struggling financially, mentally and with little support really defines what this industry can be like for some. I'm not attempting to create stigma around the music industry. We are aware of some of the issues that musicians can face, perhaps not the severity of the effects.

As you'll see from some of the musician's stories, self-funding a tour is a common practice and means that an independent musician or band can experience travelling and raise their profile in other cities and even countries. It takes planning and speaking to venues, promoters etc, it can be really exciting but tiring. Not only are individuals tested during this time, but the band dynamics can be too, we'll go into this later. Money is the biggest factor in this, and financial support is key.

I worked with a client who was a singer and popular in Japan. This was really confusing to him, but welcome. He had had experienced some success in the UK where he was from, but thanks to one single that had been used in an advert over there, he'd garnered fans and a favourable following on social media. Obviously, he wanted to take advantage of this, and he funded his own trip to Japan, planning to do some gigs, press and do some tourist stuff. After three days, he received a phone call from his mum saying that his brother had been in a car accident. His brother was hurt badly, but not critical and his mum urged him not to come home. She had been worried that his reaction would be that he wanted to come home and said she had only called because she knew he would be upset if she hadn't. He and his brother had experienced a turbulent relationship. They loved one another but argued a lot and had fallen out a year previously over a family issue. Since then, they had made up, but the client said that things were always strained between them and he had regretted how he had behaved during their falling out.

When he hung up from the conversation with his mum, he was left with strong feelings. Thinking about his brother had brought up feelings of sadness and sorrow that he had never experienced before. He was feeling home sick and strongly wanted to return home. However, he two gigs that day and a radio interview. He had spent so much money and time arranging this and let's not forget the previous years of writing, performing, recording, promoting etc. A lot had gone into his music this far and this was an amazing opportunity for him.

My point is, that despite receiving that call and all the feelings that went with it, he felt he had to carry on. He was away from home and there was pressure for him to honour his commitments. Some of the pressure was due to his own ways of thinking and some from the industry, the people he'd let down if he didn't do the gigs, if he cancelled the interview. Social media would be rife with negativity on how he'd behaved, how he'd let his fans down etc. The client had to carry this around with him. He had nobody to talk to about it, and he had no support in Japan.

He did cancel his last couple of days in Japan and missed another radio interview and an intimate televised gig. He came home early and saw his brother in hospital.

But imagine this on a larger scale, when you have hundreds of thousands of fans who have bought tickets to see you perform. There are high profile musicians who have had to cancel tours and other dates because of mental illness. Some have spoken openly about their anxiety and depression. There is a lack of empathy for these artists because they are rich and famous and what the hell have they got to be down about? Just think about what it would be like for you to feel depressed and anxious and in most cases, away from friends and family. You may feel like you want to go to your room, shut yourself in and not get up for several days. Unfortunately, you have to do a sound check at 2pm, rehearse, go over that new song and then prepare yourself physically and mentally to go out onto stage and entertain hundreds or thousands of people who have come to see you and sing along to your songs. To have to adjust to that when you're depressed is certainly not something that anyone should have to endure and the pressures from the industry sometimes mean that people don't speak up until it's too late. You read about artists who have collapsed with exhaustion or have been so anxious they've had to call off a tour, it's understandable how that can happen isn't it?

The same goes for anyone on that tour who is struggling mentally. The sound people, the assistants, the keyboard player. The pressure, the dynamics, the lifestyle, a recipe for potential demise.

Tensions between band members and crew can be a catalyst for anxiety and depression on tour. You're in close contact every day and night, living together, not always able to have regular breaks, this can lead to eruptions, arguments and even band break ups. I've spoken to band members who have been so tired of their band mates that they've literally gone AWOL for a day. Getting that much needed time away is essential, but sometimes that's not possible and that's when problems occur.

It's been well documented that bands have split up whilst on tour. They've performed their dates and then decided to call it quits once they get home. I worked with a client who was in a young independent band. They had decided to fund their own tour around America, with help from parents. They were living in an RV for 8 weeks and all the issues they had with one another were aired during that time, but only after an initial 4 weeks of bickering, falling out and actual physical fights. As a counsellor, I'm an advocate for talking if something is upsetting you, letting it out, what are you afraid of if you're not doing that? However, there had been such a build up over the past year of unresolved problems, that this explosion on tour was too much for the band to endure.

We mustn't forget here that there is a massive crew on larger tours and all the crew depend on the mental health and wellbeing of the main act. If the artist or band are suffering, everyone suffers as a result. For example, not being able to do a sound check due to a rough night or a genuine depression means that the sound check is delayed by hours sometimes. This puts a huge pressure on the crew as they literally cannot get on with their jobs and are being hassled to sort things out. The management are angry because they are losing money and wasting everyone's time. It's a domino effect and it proves that mental health impacts on everyone around. Often, the crew have been working really long hours with little break and they too are getting irritated, angry and sometimes depressed with the position they find themselves. It's important that the crew and other members of a tour get the support they need and deserve and are listened to. Sadly, with the pressure of the job, it's not always easy for them to receive that support. I want to illustrate this scenario by writing about a session with Gary, a tour manager who snapped and left a tour mid-way:

> *"I don't know where to begin, but I will say this is really hard."*
>
> *"What specifically are you finding hard?"*
>
> *"Opening up and telling someone how I feel. I lost my job because of stress and I feel ashamed when I think of what happened. I just couldn't take it anymore, I really couldn't, and it was either me or them. I know how that sounds, but it's just the way it was."*
>
> *"Why don't you start by telling me what 'it' is. You said you couldn't take 'it' anymore."*

Gary laughs, shakes his head and looks up to the ceiling.

> *God. I don't know where to start. Erm, stress, worry, pressure, constant abuse, not knowing what was going on half the time, having to listen to everyone's f*****g whim. Having to manage everyone, physically getting into the middle of a fight between the band and having to pull grown men off one another. Being forced into a situation where I had to ask one of the lighting crew to do something illegal, so we could just get on with the show. Putting him and everyone else at a huge health risk. Bloody hell, I don't know.*
>
> That sounds like a good start to exploring things. It seems like you do know.
>
> *Mmm. I hate myself for walking out when I did. We still had 31 dates left. But I genuinely don't think I'd be here if I'd stayed and I can say that from the bottom*

of my heart. It really was either me or that tour. I could feel myself spiralling and I called my wife and told her I'd have to think about what I'm doing here. I thought she'd be angry because I'd be leaving the money and I'm in legal trouble now because I had a contract, but she actually cried. She was happy I'd decided that. She had listened to me night after night complaining and bitching about everyone and everything and I think she'd had enough too. Look what it's done to all of us. God knows what's going on for the poor guy who's taken over from me.

We talked about the pressures surrounding Gary's job and how he manages them.

*"To be completely truthful, I don't think I do manage stress at all. I got on with it and brushed everything away. I knew I'd been feeling stressed and under pressure for ages before I snapped. With this business, and especially with the job I have, you must accept pressure, it's a part of everything and you can't get through the day, you can't get through an hour without it I'd say. I know other people who do what I do who feel exactly the same. When things are great, it's fun, it's exciting, it's unpredictable and entertaining and rock n f*****g role, you know? People would dream to see the things I've seen, I tell you. You name one famous rock star and I'll tell you something I've seen them do that will make you blush. But on the other hand, it is stressful, and it was just too much, too many things."*

Tell me about the day you say you 'snapped' What had led up to that point.

Gary shakes his head and laughs again.

*"Right. It was about 8 in the morning, late night the night before, think I'd got into bed at about 5. I was absolutely knackered. One of the crew banged on my door saying that one of the band had, I kid you not, defecated on another band member's guitar. The crew girl said they were screaming at each other and were threatening to kill one another. I ran to the room, I mean you could hear it when you were in the corridor. Good job we'd booked the whole floor out. They were screaming, and I mean screaming at each other and rolling around on the floor. I didn't even think about it, I dived into it and pulled the one on top off and pushed him against the wall. My heart was pounding, I was just getting through on adrenaline at this point and living in the moment, but after it hit me. What the hell was this? What was I doing? Babysitting grown f*****g men who s*** on each other's stuff? You couldn't make it up. I was seriously considering telling everyone I was quitting; this kind of stuff had been going on for months before. We'd been on the road for 4 months at this point, 80 dates, constant bloody immature crap. I'm not a counsellor, I listen to all their problems and try and deal with their s*** all the time but I couldn't do it*

anymore. I had a tour crew of great guys, great guys and they needed me to tell them what was going on, they were kept hanging all the time. They were trying to do their jobs, they were professionals. Making a living is not easy when you're on a tour like this. I've been in this game for 25 years. The crew deserve better than this."

It sounds like you've really had to deal with a lot. It sounds overwhelming at times. You mentioned not being a counsellor and having to listen to people's problems. It's making me wonder about the lack of resources available to you in terms of support and whether there's opportunity there for someone to investigate the mental health of people on tour. Something to think about.

It needs to be thought about. I genuinely believe that if there'd been someone there to help deal with their stuff, my stuff, everyone's stuff, this probably wouldn't have happened, you never know I guess.

I think this statement is significant and illustrates that above all else, mental health is at the centre of everything. Gary says he feels all the issues and his eventual demise on tour could have been avoided with support and guidance from a mental health professional.

It's not in everyone's budget to hire a mental health professional to go on tour with a band or artist, understandably. However, just to have someone to talk to, someone who can support without judgement could be really helpful. The answer doesn't have to be a permanent member of staff on tour, but it could be support in place for a few of the gigs, backstage for example, or phone sessions on tap.

From a slightly different perspective to Gary's is a band from Ireland who's lead singer I spoke to recently. He didn't want the band to be named, I asked why. He stated that he didn't want anyone to know that the band had had problems with conflict as they 'may get back together one day':

We went on tour, it was a small tour, just around the UK and that. We funded it ourselves and we'd been talking about it for a couple of years. We planned it really well, spoke to all the venues beforehand, checking it was all still on. We were really excited. We started off in Ireland, then came over to the UK, all the big cities, London, Birmingham, Manchester, loads of others.

How long had you been together at that point?

We'd been together for about 4 years at that point, but we weren't really serious for a couple of years. Talking about the tour was when we started to become more serious about it. We had loads of songs, we got in the studio, recorded a really good album, we thought. We got loads of them made, produced and we tried to get them out there, selling them at gigs.

So how did you get around while you were on tour?

Once we flew over to the UK, we hired a van and loaded all the stuff in. We had to carry all of our stuff around the airport, it was well funny. Tiring, but funny, we were all so excited it didn't matter. And then, yeah, we had the van waiting for us which was quite a good size. I mean, there was 5 of us and all our stuff, so it needed to be a good size! But, you know, like with anything, tensions started after a few weeks and we started getting irritated.

What was the first thing you remember about the tension, what started it, can you pinpoint?

*For me, it was when we got into the third or fourth week, this was meant to be about halfway through. We'd lasted pretty well until then. We weren't living in the van, we were staying in hostels in cheap hotels, we'd sorted all of that before we left. But then one of the band started getting angry saying he didn't want to stay in sh******s anymore and started shouting at the guy who'd booked the accommodation for us, one of the other members of the band. It was horrible, we were all shouting at him to calm down, must have sounded awful for anyone who could hear. In the end, he said sorry and that he was just tired and we all went out and got p*****d and the whole thing was forgotten. Then a couple of nights later, the same thing happened again but this was about the venues we'd been playing. It was the same guy making the fuss, you know? He had an idea in his head of what it was going to be and it wasn't how he thought and he was having a proper meltdown. I mean, I've know this guy for 13 years and I've never see him like this. So, we try and calm him down again, but this time it was different. It was like he was having a panic attack and he was rocking back and forth on the bed. We got him water, it was weird.*

Sounds a bit scary too, for him and for the rest of you. And did he calm down eventually?

He did, yeah, but it seemed like ages and after that, things just didn't feel the same. We were arguing on stage and stuff. You know, in the sound checks if something wasn't right. Usually we'd be chatting and agreeing on stuff, helping each other but we just weren't now. Something had changed and we didn't get it back again.

From what you were telling me, you actually split up on the tour, so how did it finally end?

"We just kept having gigs like that, and in the end one of the band walked out of the soundcheck and we all followed him and when we got outside, we just had it out. Like a proper hear to heart in a way. We didn't argue, we just all talked. We talked about how the tour wasn't what we thought it was going to be. Well, the first few weeks were, but after that it wasn't. And it wasn't just us, people weren't showing up to the gigs. I mean, we were completely responsible for everything. I don't know what you think of promoters, but I don't have a lot of faith in them to be honest and we were just let down. A few of us were feeling homesick too, I was the only one to admit that! I missed everyone, and I missed having gigs where people actually came! But, it was nice in a way, we all hugged and went and had a few drinks and it was alright. We talked about it the next day and decided not to finish the tour and to take a break, but I'm still not sure if that's still happening or if we're split up, but I think we're split up!"

You look a bit disappointed and sad when you say that.

I am disappointed. Like I said, I've known most of the guys for 13 years, we grew up together. I thought we had a bond or something, I don't know what we had, but it wasn't what I thought.

What advice would you give to any band thinking of funding themselves to go on tour?

I'd say to them that it's a great thing and really exciting, but just to be prepared for a bit of disappointment. It is hard. I don't know what we all expected but it wasn't what we got. I think we thought it was going to be a bit more glamorous. Not even glamorous, exciting and rock 'n' roll. And no matter how strong you think your friendships are, they might not be by the end of it. It sounds really depressing that doesn't it?! It's not all doom 'n' gloom, like I said, those first weeks were great. Maybe if we had been staying in the Hilton or something, things wouldn't have happened the way they did! So yeah, book yourselves in at the Hilton, make sure you've got some home comforts and just look after each other.

I felt quite emotional after this interview. I felt like something had been lost and that it was a shame. I feel deep down that the band will be OK and perhaps just need a bit of time, but that may just be the optimist in me! I've asked him to keep me posted on what happens. Wouldn't it be great if they did rekindle their friendships and the band was stronger than ever?

From this and the other tales in this chapter, I've had a strong impression that life on tour isn't all it's made out to be in the concert footage, and that the stories of groupies and glamour don't reflect reality. Life on tour can have a serious affect on everyone's mental health and again, it's important to highlight the need for support and guidance in the music industry around this and many other aspects of the musician's lifestyle.

SELF-CARE AND GUIDANCE

- Any situation where you're away from family and friends for long periods will be difficult mentally. Musicians and all members of a tour crew may experience mental health issues at some point and it's important that people share how they're feeling.

- In times where you've received bad news or are emotional after speaking to a loved one on the phone, try and get some time to look after yourself and be aware that you need to take a break from you're schedule. If this isn't possible, it needs to be made very clear to the tour manager that if you don't get the time you need, things will become very difficult for you.

- If you are the tour manager, be aware that you are finding things hard and stressful and have some time to yourself as soon as you can to breathe and close your eyes. This could be a twenty-minute coffee break on your own, but it needs to happen.

- It's becoming abundantly clear that there needs to be a provision for mental health whilst on tour and in the music industry as a whole. Let's learn from this and keep the conversation going.

9. Money

Once you start considering mental health in the music industry, hundreds of different issues come to mind. So many possibilities, factors and intricacies can contribute towards how a person feels about themselves, and how this affects their situation.

Money is a huge therapeutic issue, how does it relate to mental health and the music industry?

When 'Helpmusicians' did their survey on depression and anxiety amongst musicians, some of these musicians said that to be a musician meant that they were living in the back of a van, going to gigs for no pay or very low pay which just covers the cost of petrol. Most musicians want to make a living out of music, pay bills, buy food, support their families. This requires an income and not all musicians will have the opportunity to make money to allow them to do these things. Most musicians will be aware of this but will be striving to do so constantly. Some professional musicians may get irregular pay and have to pick up other work when they're in-between music jobs. Classical musicians I've spoken to sometimes feel they have long periods between paid gigs and therefore must take other work such as teaching to pay bills. They then feel pressure to take any work that comes even if it means leaving their family on tour for long periods which can lead to anxiety and depression.

Some musicians may want to get on the road and promote their music, get on stage and play their material to as many audiences as possible. One musician whom you will read about in their own experience explained that he has self-funded a tour around the UK without any support financially from any label. And this is where the 'day job' comes in. If you're not making a living out of your music, you must have a job during the day to pay the bills and fund your music career. If you want to record, you need the money, if you want to produce the CD and have hundreds of copies printed off, you need to pay for this. If you want to rehearse you have to pay for a room unless you know someone who is happy for you to use their cellar or garage. This is not an easy industry, but so many people choose this lifestyle. Why?

When I asked the following client if I could write about her for the book, she was really sweet and enthusiastic about it. I think this works better as a story rather than a session transcript. We'll call her Jennifer.

Jennifer was 17 when she realized that she wanted to try and make a living out of her music. She went to high school and studied GCSE Music amongst other subjects and she was an accomplished pianist. Her parents wanted her to go to university and study journalism and it was something she was always passionate about, Jennifer was quite happy to apply. However, when it came to the summer before Jennifer was supposed to go, things changed. Jennifer says she remembers sitting at the piano at a friend's house, her friend's asking her to play something as they frequently did. She says that there was a new friend there with a guitar. Jennifer recalled him being really confident in getting out the guitar, playing Jimi Hendrix, and tunes from other bands they all loved like Radiohead, Stereophonics etc. She says she started playing along really nervously at first, but eventually they were really jamming together. Jennifer says she thinks of the look on everyone's faces as they stared, impressed and admiring. Afterwards, her friends were congratulating her and telling her she needed to do that more often. Jennifer agreed. She felt it had opened up her world and there was no going back.

Jennifer broke the news to her parents that she wouldn't be studying journalism, they were concerned but supportive. She applied to study for music degrees and spent 3 years getting a 1st in Music at Durham University.

She had made a lot of contacts during her time at university, continuously being asked to play with, jazz, funk, soul and rock bands. Jennifer says she was confident in many styles of music and her tastes were very eclectic, but felt that her talents really lied in funk and soul. She remembers her parents visiting and coming to see one of her gigs. She laughed as she told me they were on the front row, dancing away and cheering 'yeah Jennifer! That's our daughter!'.

Jennifer says that she didn't get paid a lot for the gigs she played during those 3 years. The going rate for a gig was around £50 and being a student, she was always grateful and enjoyed the work. Jennifer maintains that it was always her plan to make as many contacts as she could and try and work as a session musician after university. Fortunately, this plan came to fruition while she was coming to the end of her degree, she was approached by an agency who booked session musicians. Jennifer recalls her first paid job as a session musician as being 'wonderful'. She was paid a hefty sum for a day's work and was obviously thirsty for more. The agency seemed respectful, easy to work with and very connected, Jennifer was hopeful for the future. There were times where the work wasn't as frequent, and she found it difficult to know where her next pay day would be coming from. These were difficult times and Jennifer said she was really struggling and signed on for job seekers allowance during this period.

She was on benefits for 3 months until a big paid job came along, it broke the draught and gave Jennifer a little faith back that she was doing the right thing job wise. It was a job playing with a major band on tour, a soul band whom Jennifer really loved and she says she was over the moon at the prospect. She soon learnt all of their songs from every album and every solo, she was excited. Jennifer says the tour proved to be difficult, but that she enjoyed it for the most part. She says that sometimes the accommodation wasn't what it had been made out to be beforehand but that she was usually so tired, she didn't care as long as there was a bed to sleep in.

Jennifer toured for almost 16 weeks with the band and she was hopeful that they'd use her again for their next tour and possibly a recording. Her mind was racing at all the opportunities that would come her way now. Word gets around in the music industry, other artists would hear about her and she'd have regular work!

This wasn't to be, not at first. It took Jennifer a couple of years to get to a point where she was almost booked up with little gaps, but she says there are still times of 'draught' even now. Jennifer did say that after the first tour, she spent 8 weeks trying to get the money that she'd earnt. There were apparently issues with the payment that Jennifer could not control, and she chased the person dealing with it every day. During this time, Jennifer had to sign on to job seekers allowance again because she couldn't pay her rent or buy food. Her work as a musician had been flourishing and then died off. Jennifer said that she did suffer from periods of depression, especially the times where the work had been irregular, and she had had to turn to benefits. She started questioning whether she was good enough, whether she had made the right decision, should she just give it all up? She was incredibly anxious at times about whether or not she could pay her rent, what her options would be, possibly having to move back home and admit to her parents that things hadn't worked out the way she'd hoped. Jennifer said she emailed and called every agency she could think of during these 'draughts'. She said she called all of the contacts she'd made during university but that nobody could help. She felt like she was begging, Jennifer said this is sometimes how things are with musicians and that it's accepted, and nobody ever made her feel bad for doing it, but that she'd felt very low.

The issue of money within the music industry isn't just relating to the money the artist or musician earns, it's to do with what goes on behind the scenes. The record labels who have the money to put behind an artist or band need certain guarantees first that aren't always easy to give. They are potentially putting hundreds of thousands of pounds behind these up and coming musicians and so a lot must go into these acts to ensure they will meet up to everyone's expectations. This means image needs to be just right, music needs to be honed and perfected. The producers and mixers need to be among the best and everyone needs to be on the same page. The social media campaign may cost a fortune, but we're all aware that this is what's needed for success in these times where it's not just about the music.

I spoke to Nahari, a singer who was signed by a major label in 2003, but who was 'shelved' because there wasn't enough money to support her campaign:

I just wanted to make the music, but they kept telling me it wasn't the right time for me. That's the total opposite of what they said when they first signed me" Nahari recalls. "I found out a year later that this department didn't have the budget for me and that the project was dead, and nobody bothered to tell me.

Nahari said this didn't stop her, that she went on to make music without the label, but that she fell into a spiral of depression for a few months afterwards. *I felt sick, like I'd been totally duped and the fact that they all just kept stringing me along and not telling me the truth, I felt like getting a loan and saying 'here f****g have this! Now can we just get on with it!*

I tried to get hold of the people at the label Nahari was signed to, nobody wanted to comment. I did however talk to Jacob who works in artist development for a label based in Denmark.

Sadly, it's a tale that's only to common in the music industry. There's a big influx of artists because the larger labels want to sign people who are like another, bigger artist. For example, Ed Sheeran is the biggest pop star on the planet right now, but back when he first started to become big, all the labels were signing little Ed Sheerans. They pay the money to 'reserve' the artists in some ways so nobody else can sign them, and then don't have the intentions or the money to see it through."

This must be so hard for musicians who are being told that all of their dreams are about to come true, and then be completely let down by the very label that signed them.

Mike was in an Indie band from 1994-1998. He says they were signed by a record label but that the money they were given as an advance for recording their album and other expenses didn't even 'cut the sides'.

We were absolutely on cloud 9, it was the best news that we could have had. Anyone in a band is lying if they say they'd turn down a record deal if it was offered to them. We worked really hard for two years, writing, rehearsing, getting together most evenings to play but also to go over who we'd sent stuff out to, where we wanted to gig and how to make that happen. It was a lot of work as well as our jobs. One of us was at uni and missed some of the rehearsal, but he dropped uni once we'd signed. I think he was thinking 'what's the point in uni when I'm going to be rich!!' but it didn't quite happen like that.

We were given about £80,000 which was more money than we'd ever had before, and we were really grateful. The spokesperson for the label explained that this was our first album and that once we'd shown we could sell and were bankable, we'd be making a lot more. We all believed him, all wanted to make money and just be musicians. That was why we were in it, why else? Once we'd hired a studio, paid the producer, mixer, masterer, all the rest and then had all photos taken, artwork done, CD's printed out etc, we were left with about £50,000. There were 5 of us in the band, that was roughly £10,000 for us all to live on. We were asked to go on tour which was included in the money we'd already been given, so we were actually struggling after a year of this and it wasn't at all what we expected. We weren't in control of anything, we were told where to record, who to use, which photographer and we had to trust that our manager was making the right choices and how much everything had cost was the truth. It's all changed now, but people who think that getting in a band and working hard will make them rich are going to be very disappointed. I've met young lads in bands today who think that they're great, that's really good to be confident, but they need to manage their expectations on the money front because I'm telling you, there isn't money in the music industry until you're at a level where you're touring with a well known, profitable act and the label are prepared to put some money in you.

Do you agree with Mike? I think managing expectations is so important in all of these mental health and music issues. Especially when it comes to making it and money. There are so many expectations put on musicians and that musicians put on themselves to be able to make a living and in some cases being so rich they can buy their parents a mansion. We've all seen MTV's Cribs.

From my own experience, you can have financial control to a degree if you work hard, put some money in yourself and know how to market your band, gigs etc. This is crossing over into changes in the industry a little, but with regards to money, within my band, we have put on our own 'pop up' gigs and funded a bar, hired the place and charged for tickets. Once we've paid the beautiful accompanying string players, we have had a little money left. Now, if we were to do that once or twice a week, we'd be heading to a place where we could make a humble living.

Could this be the future of money in the industry? Gigging is where we get told most of the money is. People often state that 'there's no money in albums anymore, gigging is where it's at'. This may be the case, but albums are still relevant and if little else, having the CD to sell at the gig is great promotion.

If you're an independent artist, it is possible to make money by putting on your own gigs. Many artists including Heidi Dewhurst, who wrote a piece for this book hire regular places to put on acoustic gigs for themselves and or other acts. This is not enough to make a living, but it's a start and it gives the acts an outlet to express and a place to be seen and most importantly heard by others.

We discussed how changes in the music industry can affect mental health, and the money is definitely a part of that. If the future of music is independent artists and cottage industries does mean it that there will be more money in smaller amounts being exchanged? Will musicians be satisfied with having a more humble career, but with more control and independence. It was stated that some independent musicians are actually turning away offers from major labels because they don't want to do down that route, they want to maintain their autonomy and have the power over their creativity and all other aspects of their careers. But maintaining that level of autonomy and 'staying independent' does come with a cost. If artist and musicians are turning away offers from major labels, they are also turning away the chance to make potentially larger amounts of money.

I see why artists are turning away the majors after my own experience. But it's important that we don't lose our way with this and still be making sure that the music that deserves to be heard does get heard. I'm not saying that if you're independent you aren't going to be heard, the contrary seems to be happening now, but we need to be careful we aren't turning down opportunities to give people a platform on a massive scale and give a voice to people who need it, the potential to reach a massive audience is something to think about.

Nahari has an excellent point. We discuss Kendrick Lamar in the chapter on Race and discrimination, in that he has used money to help the people around him. Dr Dre has put millions of dollars into the community of Compton to regenerate it and give the young people a chance to shine and release themselves from socio economic decline. After selling his streaming company to Apple, he became the first Hip Hop billionaire. Isn't there something in that he could in some respects, free himself from the struggles of his own past by helping the community he hailed from and give others the opportunities power and self-worth?

There's a long way to go in managing expectations around money in the music industry. Due to the different levels of success, there is such a leap from one level to another. It brings us back to worth and 'making it' in many ways. Do we put too much emphasis on our self-worth as musicians through how much money we are making? If we aren't making any money, is it then just a hobby?

A musician and a working musician are not the same, however, they are both still musicians. A working musician is a professional or semi-professional musician, that is the difference. I remember when I was younger, speaking to musicians who were on the dole, on benefits. They were saying that people used to laugh at them and say 'well, if you're not making money out of it, you're not a musician'. This always confused me, I didn't understand it. They were clearly confused with the 'professional' labelling, but a musician is a musician whether they're professional or picking up their violin whenever they get the chance.

These same musicians were the ones who used to berate other musicians if they had a job, saying they obviously weren't serious or they'd give up their jobs and 'do music full time'. Such a strange statement, that you aren't serious about something if you don't give up your job for it. Do others feel like this? I spoke to a singer songwriter I met at an open mic. I asked her specifically about this statement to see if she had any experience of this:

I've been a singer songwriter for about 12 years and I also have a job. I can think of a handful of people who have said that I can't be serious about it if I still have a job. I have a job because I am serious about it! How do these magical musicians who don't have jobs and who are serious about music find the money to fund their music? How do they make recordings? Pay photographers? I just don't understand that kind of mentality at all. It's one of those where afterwards you have loads of things you want to say and wish you'd thought of! But seriously, what are they talking about? How do you justify that statement at all? Maybe they feel like real troubadours if they sit around and play music all day, like they're authentic, but I'd honestly like to ask them what kind of musicians they are. I fund my music, because I want people to hear it. Maybe they'd think that was selling out too. Maybe in their eyes, you're only a true musician if you suffer and your music is only for you. I kind of get that, but unfortunately money is the way that I feel good about where I am because I'm able to pay for stuff, able to get my music heard because it deserves to be.

I asked her to expand a bit more about the positive effects of having money to fund music.

I work and yeah, my job is just OK. Sometimes I feel like I'm helping people,

> *making some kind of small difference. But when I don't, it's alright, because I have my voice, my guitar, which I paid for, and my mic, which I paid for; I can get in my car and drive to venues and get out and get in front of a stage and open my sole up and that helps me. That makes it all worth it. I don't accept that I'm not a real musician, or a serious musician because I work. It's rubbish. There are definite positives to being able to put money into my music. For one, I feel really good about myself when I write a song, practice, make it sounds great, and then go into the studio and record it. I can listen to the thing I have made, the song I've written. That is a good feeling. If I'm feeling crap about myself, which everyone does from time to time, I can plan and save to put some money into music. My money may not come from music -yet, but I'm not sorry for having a job and I'm not going to be made to feel bad for having some self-respect.*

There's some anger there, and understandably so. If someone told you you weren't serious about something and judged you, it wouldn't feel good.

As we can see looking back over this chapter, money holds so much power within the music industry, no matter what level you happen to be at. Despite the clichéd dreams to 'make it big' in the music industry and land a million-dollar deal, some musicians are actually turning away from that despite the promise of huge opportunities and money beyond their wildest dreams.

Some musicians had that dream and then watched it pass them by as the record labels ran out of funding for them, some had money and then watched it get dwindled away, out of their control. And others are working to fund their music, having the day job, and then referring to music as their second job. So much around this issue, so many perspectives and experiences of money in the music industry.

SELF-CARE AND GUIDANCE

- If you have been working professionally or semi-professionally as a musician and are having difficulties with receiving what's owed to you, there are different agencies and unions that can help such as The Musicians' Union, The ISM- Incorporated Society Of Musicians and Helpmusicians.

- Money is such a massive issue in all walks of life. Remember that it doesn't mean letting go of your dreams if you don't have money to fund your music. You may have to make a few adjustments, do the things you know you can do with little money. Write, perform, those things are free and will help you realize that you're doing this for you.

- There is no shame in making money in different ways if you aren't able to make money out of music at this time. It's common for musicians to think they're 'selling out' if they join a function band, that it's not genuine music in some way. That's not the case. Music is music, if you enjoy it and are getting paid, isn't that making it by the definition of what making it is to most musicians?

- If you are working all day and getting home and starting your '2nd job' make sure you give yourself some time off, an evening, a day a week so that it's not always about this one thing. Again, what are you doing this for? If you burn out, where's the enjoyment in that and what is it doing to you mentally? Keep questioning that, it's so much better if you're well and able to keep yourself healthy.

10. Performance Anxiety

When I was just starting out as a young singer in my late teens, I knew how I came across on stage, but I found it so hard to change. I was very stiff, I didn't project a lot of emotion at all in my body or face. My voice was lovely, but I always felt inadequate on stage.

Now, I'm a lot more confident and I enjoy performing, but that younger me and inner critic is still in there. "Why don't you talk more? Banter with the audience!" These thoughts make me feel insecure- self doubt creeps in and I start to worry about how I'm coming across. I know exactly what's happening, I just want to be myself- why can't 'myself' be better?

I deliver performance anxiety workshops, working with people on different parts of the anxiety scale. I've worked with clients who suffer from extreme anxiety, where they become incredibly sick before a performance and start shaking, vomiting and freeze with fear. This is sometimes experienced by musicians, but also professionals who want to be able to deliver a speech or a talk. On the other end of the scale is mild anxiety, musicians who feel shaky and want to improve their performance and enjoy it rather than worry about how they're coming across. I encourage them to talk about the feelings and what they're afraid of. What's the worst thing that can happen for you in this situation? Is that likely to happen? What would happen if it did?

One client I worked with said that she felt she didn't put any emotion into her performance. Again, this completely resonated with the younger me. We discussed the feelings; she was worried she was being judged, she felt embarrassed if she closed her eyes or smiled when she sung a certain phrase. She had written the song at home, put experiences and emotions in there. She had hummed the melody and sung it to herself and thought carefully about how she wanted the emotions to come across to the audience. However, this was becoming lost in translation when it was time to perform. She said that when she was a teenager, she would send her parents out of the house when she wanted to write and sing. They would oblige.

After talking to her for a while, we discovered that her family didn't share their emotions, didn't talk about how they felt and laughed about everything in order to cope and now it was their strategy to deal with things. There was love and warmth, but she said it was embarrassing when it came to "icky feelings stuff" It's no surprise then that she felt she couldn't express her emotions on stage if she hadn't been brought up to express her emotions with others. We talked about trying to take a small phrase of her song and deciding that she was going to sing it a certain way, that this might make her anxious but that it was part of the development. Next time she performed one of her songs, she laughed a little at a certain phrase and the audience laughed with her. She said she felt warm and satisfied and was surprised at how easy it had been and natural it had felt once she saw how the audience had reacted. Her anxiety lifted a little, but lets not forget that a little bit of nerves can actually be useful when performing, producing adrenalin and helping you to focus.

It's not just independent musicians who suffer from performance anxiety, it can affect artists who have been performing for years and nobody would ever believe that they suffer because of their outward appearance and abilities. Carly Simon has gone on record saying that she has suffered from stage fright so badly that she has collapsed on stage. Other times, she has invited audience members on stage to help her and support her. Barbara Streisand famously didn't do any live performances for almost 30 years because she was so affected by a performance where she's suffered from anxiety and had forgotten lyrics.

Over a year ago, I worked with a client who said he was 'crippled' with performance anxiety and needed to work through it and try and come to terms with why he had such a reaction to performing. Callum loved playing his guitar and writing songs, he said he always got such a great reaction from people when he performed his songs but couldn't get over his performance anxiety:

> There must be something in the performing that's significant for you to keep carrying on.
>
> *Yeah, I love it. I know that sounds weird because I'm here for performance anxiety issues, but I do. I just hate the fact I feel sick before I go on and spend the hour before vomiting. Nobody would know though. I think and I've been told that I look really confident on stage.*
>
> What do you feel is behind the anxiety? A fear of being judged? A fear something

will go wrong?

Both of those, and also just the fact that it's really real if you know what I mean? There's no hiding from it, it's me and I'm showing everyone who I am. It's sort of power, but not when it makes me feel like that. The problem I have is about an hour before when I realise I'm going on stage and I get proper worked up. My heart beats fast, I start to feel really sick, most of the time I am sick for a bit.

It sounds really worrying for you, but that you're very good at hiding it.

Oh yeah, definitely. I make sure nobody is in the loo before I start being sick. And then I come out and look find, even though I don't feel it. But I know it's worth it, because I love my music and I do think I'm talented. I love people telling me they think I'm good, I love it when people are really quiet during a slow song and I can hear how clear my voice is.

You seem confident talking about your abilities, what are you worried about in terms of being judged or something going wrong?

Callum laughs *That's the thing. When I was in high school, I had to get up in front of everyone at assembly and do this thing on my own. It was like a speech for the topic we were doing in class, but the teacher asked me because she thought mine was really good. I remember feeling so ill, for days before. I was terrified. I couldn't speak properly, I did really badly and everyone was looking at me, whispering and sniggering. How I feel when I go on stage now might have something to do with that, even though it's not at all the same situation.*

Callum and I discussed this further, that now he performs because he enjoys it but also to prove to his younger self that he can do it.

It sounds like your younger self is trying to sabotage you, telling you that you can't do it although you know you can.

I would agree with that but I don't understand how it could have affected me so much without me knowing. I think some of it is trying to protect myself too. If I get anxious and sick, isn't it my way of telling myself that I shouldn't be going out there?

Absolutely, that's a great analysis. But we know that it's incorrect so you don't need that protection anymore. It's about teaching that inner child that you no longer need to be protected, that you've got it and it's all good.

I suggested that once we'd finished our work together, that Callum tries some CBT. I'm not sure of the outcome of that, but it can be great for anxiety in certain environments and in creating strategies for people to deal with their anxiety in the moment.

After being lucky enough to see a gig of his in Manchester this year, I asked singer songwriter Hak Baker if he had ever suffered from performance anxiety:

*Yeahhhh all the time. I get shaky and s**t, then I drink. It don't help quick enough but it does eventually. Get confident though. But nowadays I'm less anxious finally.*

Here's an artist who's at the start of his career, a very promising one, receiving acclaim from fans and critics alike. Even he suffers from performance anxiety. It definitely didn't come across during the gig, although there were times where you did see emotion and vulnerability, as he apologised for becoming emotional during certain songs. It was a true testament to authenticity and talent of Hak Baker, but also the acceptance of himself; that he allowed himself to become emotional in front of an audience, that it was OK.

It would appear that this is one of the troubles concerning performance anxiety, that we're exposing ourselves to too much. Will it be OK? Will I survive it? As with the client earlier, I ask 'what are you afraid of?' For some musicians, it isn't a cognitive process, it's simply a feeling so overpowering that it eclipses all else. I spoke to Daniel, a musician from Leeds who says he used to suffer from performance anxiety until he '"decided to get over it" and did:

> *Performance anxiety, or stage fright as I used to call it was devastating to me. I knew I was talented, I knew that I wanted to be in a band, write songs, be part of something creative and be with other people who wanted to do the same thing. I spent ages building up the courage to put out an ad which I did. It worked out really well. I mean, there were a few dodgy people who replied but luckily they all went away without being too miffed! I did meet the right people. We clicked and started writing. Actually, one of the band already had some songs that were pretty good, they were a brilliant starting point because it meant that we could get right into it and figure out our sound. I was fine in rehearsals because I was comfortable with these guys. The environment was calm, relaxed. There was a bit of pressure but I was much more sorted in that situation. But then we had our first gig coming up and I just broke down one night and I kept saying I couldn't do it. The others were so nice about it and tried to talk to me about it. They calmed me down and we did the gig and I just couldn't cope with it at all. I got through it, but I swore I'd never do it again. That really disappointed me, I felt I'd let them down, but also let myself down because it was something I*

*really wanted to do. I'd had a panic attack basically, and I didn't want another one. All through the gig, I was sweating, couldn't look at the audience. I barely looked up at all, I needed to communicate with the others, but I found it so hard and I just wanted to be sick. I hear people say adrenaline takes over and you just get on with it. That must have happened, because I swear, I do not know how I got through it. Like before, the others tried to talk me round and I just kept saying I didn't want to do it. In the end, they convinced me to do a gig because they said it would be so small that it would be like a rehearsal and there was no worries and they'd look after me. I agreed, it was a small gig but there were still people there! That was the problem, other people looking at me, watching my playing, what I was doing, and me thinking I was crap and shouldn't be on the stage. Anyway, I swore again that I wouldn't do it again and just thought, 'well this isn't for me' but it didn't feel right and I didn't really want that. I was telling myself it wasn't for me, and that wasn't fair on anyone. I was missing out on something I wanted to do and I started to get angry and that was when I thought "Right, stop this, get over yourself. Nobody's bothered what you're doing, they're listening to the songs and watching everyone and f*** what everyone else thinks anyway!" It was really hard but I pushed myself to do it, and I kept arranging gigs, I wanted to prove that I could do it. And to be honest, each and every one of those gigs has been torture, but I've been glad I've done them when we've come off the stage and it's been a good gig. I'm still angry with myself for feeling like this, maybe I need some counselling! But you know, at least I'm doing the thing I wanted to do and not letting anything stop me.*

Barbra Streisand

Barbra Streisand is one of the best known and best loved vocalists and actresses of all time. She has one 10 Grammy Awards, 9 Golden Globes, 2 Academy Awards, Emmy Awards and Tony awards. She is still regarded as an artist that stands apart with her extensive vocal range and the feeling and emotion she puts into her songs. She found success in the 1960's as a recording artist and has enjoyed a career spanning over 50 years.

However, despite this outstanding success within the music industry, Barbra Streisand has stated frequently over the years that she suffers from performance anxiety. At a concert in Central Park in 1967, she forgot the words to a song and has reported that she uses a tele prompter at gigs now so there's no chance of this happening again.

The anticipation of forgetting the words and the expectation around what will happen if she does seems to drive Barbra Streisand's performance anxiety, seemingly stemming from this concert. She felt embarrassed, humiliated and unprofessional. This will have then carried on for the rest of her careers, always haunting her, creeping in before concerts resulting in self doubt and criticism.

In 1995, after she had won 5 Emmys for her HBO concert special, she told ABC news:

"I think fear is a great energiser, it pushes you into things and without it, you might not push yourself to certain heights. So, you have to see the positive side of fear and I think that's what I try to do because I don't like to be so stifled by my own problems and therefore I thought it was an interesting challenge to go out there and face the music." She went on to say:

"I think it's very important to have self-doubt. One part of me wishes I was more confident and the other part of says 'no' it's a great balancer to the part of me that does have confidence. It's about humanity, it's about being able to have compassion, to identify with people. I no longer look at it as such a negative thing."

It's no wonder, reading about people's experiences within this chapter that another label for Performance anxiety is 'stage fright'. When you're in the music industry, that's exactly what it is. You're frightened to go on stage for whatever reason, and that fear can dictate what you do from that moment. Barbra Streisand stated that she uses the fear, that she feels it makes her more able to identify with people, and in part, takes away the gloss and glamour and makes her 'real'.

Having an understanding of performance anxiety as stage fright has certainly enriched my work as a counsellor. Behind most anxiety is fear, and it's getting to the root of some of the causes that will help the individual get to grips with their performance and learn strategies to cope and start to enjoy being on stage.

SELF-CARE AND GUIDANCE

- I'm a big believer in getting to the root of your problems and taking the time to find out where your anxiety comes from. This might take a while in some cases but it's worth exploring isn't it?
- Practically, in the moment, box breathing can really help. Breath in for 4 seconds, breathe out for 4 seconds, this will help centre and calm you.
- Accept that you will feel nervous and anxious, it's happening so try and work with it! If you try and fight it and resist, you risk increasing the chances of a panic attack.
- Use the emotions you feel, you're passionate about what you're doing so don't try to repress it.
- Everyone feels anxious to an extent when performing, whether it's musically, giving a talk or doing a wedding speech, nerves can be good and the adrenalin can improve your performance.
- Practice, be as familiar with the material as possible. However, try not to practice immediately before a performance, if anything goes wrong, it may stay with you until you go on stage, increasing anxiety.
- Focus on your stance, posture, body language.
- What are you engaging with as you perform? What do you want to put across? Why is this important to you? What are you saying with your music?

11. Discrimination and Exploitation when it comes to Race

11. Discrimination and Exploitation when it comes to Race

Whilst speaking to musicians about this book, a clear theme was coming to the surface, especially around the musicians from ethnic minorities. Having to prove yourself, always having to work harder than everyone else and always feeling like you need to fit into a stereotype to feel like you have to sell your music.

Some of the mental health issues which can arise within discrimination and exploitation within the music industry are clear. From the people I've spoken to, they largely manifest from discrimination.

I spoke to a musician about some of his experiences and how they've effected his mental health:

> *Everyone wanted a black drummer when I first started out. It was cool, it looked good and it meant that they got more black fans. Sounds obvious, but heh, it's the way it worked, still is. I'll always have work as a drummer, but it doesn't mean I haven't faced discrimination. Being black is always going to be an issue. It's always going to be the first thing that people see, and I do feel that it's the reason I do or don't get chosen for a gig. Either someone will think it's cool to have a token black man in an indie band, or they'll want the skinny white guy. I've played in loads of different bands in my time, I like any music that challenges me, but it will always be there, just like it will for you to be a*

white woman. It's always the first thing. Whether you think it or not.

I do feel depressed a lot of the time at the moment, I've told you why that is. This that I'm talking about now is something else. I feel really frustrated about it and I don't think I realized how much until now. I was just getting on with it.

I had a call day before yesterday from someone asking me to be on a TV show I've been on before, but the person who called me, I've known for years. I was excited by it, I like the band. But then he dropped in 'they needed someone who looked edgy'. Now, look at me. Do I look edgy? I mostly wear jeans and t-shirts. I don't have tattoos, piercings, anything like that. So, what do you think was edgy? The fact I'm black. After I'd put the phone down, I just felt so bad. I said yes, but now I'm asking myself why and it's bothering me a lot more than it usually would. This kind of thing happens all the time, so why am I thinking about it so much now?

I do think these issues they're affecting me now because I'm getting older, more experience. I am feeling depressed because of stuff that's going on as you know, but I think this is just making it worse, suddenly seeing how I've been treated really. I'm grateful for all the work I've had, course, but I think about what career I'd have if I was a different colour. It's starting to get me down because I am proud, and I love the drums, I love my life mostly, it's like I've been walking around in the dark and someone's turned the light on and I've seen things for what they really are.

The connection between race and mental health in the music industry is far spread, whilst interviewing Nahari, she started speaking about how she had found being a young, Asian woman in the music industry so far.

How many successful Asian musicians can you name? How many successful Asian female musicians can you name? M.I.A? in the pop music genre, there are very few women. I have no role models in pop. I could name you a hundred Asian musicians doing Indian music, I grew up with some of that around the house or around my grandparent's houses, but that's not my jam. I want strong, Asian pop stars in the charts with Little Mix and Coldplay. I grew up thinking I shouldn't be doing this, that it wasn't the place for me, that there was no place for me. I had to fight to do this and had so much to prove, I had to keep convincing people that I was good, that they needed to give me a chance.

Nina Simone

Nina Simone started out in music as Eunice Waymon. As a young child, she had played in church and a member of the audience saw her and offered lessons. Nina had a real talent for music and specialised in classical pieces, her family approved of this. She enrolled in Julliard and later applied for a prestigious music school in Philadelphia. She was reportedly turned away despite an excellent audition and always put it down to racial discrimination, something which she carried with her throughout life.

To make money, she changed her name to Nina Simone and played nightclubs to make ends meet. Her religious family told her she was playing 'the devils music'.

One nightclub told her she would have to sing as that's what the audience and clientele of the club were used to. This launched her career as a jazz, blues and gospel artist. Many of the musicians who worked with Nina Simone described her as a genius. Liz Garbus who directed the documentary 'What Happened Miss Simone?' Said this during an interview with Elle magazine:

"The way she would weave in standards and change them and use her training-fugue and counterpoint and all these different things from classical music- her mind was clearly able to operate on a lot of different levels."

I enjoyed watching the documentary on Netflix, I learnt a lot. However, one thing did strike me from the point of view of a mental health professional, I felt in some ways, Liz Garbus was saying that Nina was a 'difficult' woman and therefore in some ways was to blame for the way she was treated in life; to blame for the abuse, rejection, it didn't seem to explore what it must have been like for her as a black female growing up and experiencing discrimination. I also found it hard to swallow that her abuser, her ex-husband had been asked to be interviewed, to talk about what he did and described her as yes, 'difficult'. The title of the documentary also bothers me. She was responsible for so much positivity within music and during the civil rights movement. One of the key figures in raising awareness of rights for black people and fighting to be heard. Yes, she had mental health issues, but does this need to be the focus of the entire documentary, that something 'went wrong' with her?

Nina Simone was known to the people around her as having an angry temperament and being prone to outbursts. She was physically abusive to her daughter who ended up moving away from her to live with her father. Nina also experienced strong feelings of self-hatred around her looks and voice and exhibited inexplicably self-destructive behaviour. In an infamous clip of Nina on stage performing at the Montreux jazz festival in 1976, she seemed to disassociate completely with where was as tears started to fill her eyes. She sat staring into space. It seemed that she was consumed with depression at that point. Like so many, I would have loved to have spoken to Nina Simone about her mental health and to have found out what life was like from her childhood onwards; where the anger came from, the hurt, the need to abuse, the depression and self-hatred. I'll never get that chance to do that, but I think it's important to be aware of her struggles and the challenges that faced her, but also the massive impact she had on the world around her.

Here's a transcript from a recent radio interview with rap musician Kendrick Lamar in which he opens up about the feelings of depression he's felt within the music industry:

> Host- Did the industry cause that?
>
> Kendrick- *Not the industry, just the change. When you're around so many different faces, faces that you don't quite understand, meeting different people, things are going on back home. It's out of your control to handle.*
>
> Host- People would think that that would take you away, you know? The money, the lifestyle, you're able to take a lot of people that would usually be from the hood and give them another chance, take them to places they wouldn't usually see.
>
> Kendrick- *Yeah, you can, but you can't take everybody. There's still stuff going on, I still got family in Compton. I can't put a million dollars in their pocket and say, 'you're home now' all I can do is put them in positions where they can fend for themselves.*

It wouldn't be right to talk about race and mental health within the music industry without talking about Compton and south-central L.A, a place where a lot of rappers talk about in their music and a catalyst for a lot of the issues that can cause mental health issues.

In the Netflix documentary The Defiant Ones and the film Straight Outta Compton, Dr Dre's life is talked about before, during and after NWA. Within both, the murder of Dr Dre's brother is discussed, that he found out while they were on a tour bus.

One of the other members of the group heard him crying at the back of the bus. The glamorous side of the 'gangsta' lifestyle is often portrayed in music videos and in a lot of the lyrics in rap music, but there aren't often a lot of tears shown. The conflict between members of the band, especially around the time when there were tensions between their manager and rapper Ice Cube are enough to show that there were major stresses. Ice Cube felt he couldn't stay in the group if their manager remained, and Eazy E, the founding member of the band wouldn't allow the manager to be ousted.

It's a wonderful thing that the group were able to have the outlet for issues that were affecting them and the people around them in Compton, especially with the controversial song 'F*** tha Police'. They felt harassed by the police, as many black people in America, and the UK do. They felt out of control, helpless and hopeless.

Some musicians have no problem with 'exposing' their mental health issues, and the times where they've struggled and even felt suicidal. Lil Wayne, a 35-year-old rapper from Louisiana during time in prison in 2010 confessed that he had felt depressed:

"I ended up thinking about all types of shit. One thing that stood out was how I've never been this close to suicide before. It's truly a new reality for me."

However, in an interview in 2016, Lil Wayne stated *"I have never experienced racism-that's still a thing?"* This caused a massive backlash by other members of the music industry and the public. A few months later, Lil Wayne explained that he had been saved by a white police officer when he accidentally shot himself. *"Yeah, he was a cop, and my life was saved by a white man. I don't know what racism is."* Lil Wayne has spoken about racism frequently, and has a more positive and brighter outlook than some of his peers, saying that his fans have always just been everybody and he has never been exposed to racism. Is that refreshing? That a black artist feels so at ease and included that he can honestly state he hasn't experienced racism? The backlash he faced for his views were understandable. Lil Wayne was being incredibly naïve, and some would argue offensive, but from his personal experience, racism does not exist.

In 2014, the anti-stigma organization Time to Change did a survey of black and minority ethnic (BME) people with mental health issues. 93% of people said that they had experienced discrimination because of their mental health struggles. The researchers had this to say about the findings: *"Discrimination as a result of mental ill health is reported across a wide range of everyday activities. There are some slight variations across ethnic groups, but the overall picture is constant: discrimination is everywhere."*

So how do we relate this to the music industry? The musician earlier on in the chapter had clearly been a victim of repeated profiling concerning his image and the types of jobs he was being offered as a musician. I was fortunate enough to meet a wonderful musician who had experienced bullying and discrimination at work, claiming that race had a major factor in the experiences she had. Jayne wrote this for the book based on her experiences:

I'm a classical musician. I play in a number of orchestras. Around two years ago, bullying started, and it affected me so badly that I had to quit my work. I strongly believe I was discriminated against for being black. There were many witnesses, some came forward when I was going to tribunal, some chose not to, and I respect that. Many of these witnesses were my friends and were disgusted by how I was being treated. One of them went to the media about it. It was someone in power in the orchestra. They came in after about two years of me being there. They were new, fresh, wanted to stir things up, make their mark. I'm quite a disciplined player, I didn't take to them well at all, but I really did try. I'm a professional and I wanted to please everyone and do the best job I could. Then after around 8 months, there was a massive concert and this person took me aside and told me they thought my playing had been 'less than impressive' and asked me if there were any problems. They acted quite concerned, I told them no, I was astounded and just couldn't believe it. They told me if I didn't improve that they'd ask the 2nd to take my seat and I would be relegated, that's how it felt.

I asked the others, you know, 'do you think my playing has been less than impressive?' they all shook their heads, couldn't believe it either. My playing apparently didn't improve. I went to a union as nobody else agreed with this person. I sought help. Someone at the union asked me if I thought it was anything to do with race, I said no but then my friend pointed out that this person had made a comment once which I'd forgotten about where they said 'someone like you doesn't usually like this kind of music do they?' The meeting with the union really alerted me to the fact that he could be racist, and I watched out for it, we all did. One of my friends even kept a diary of what the person said to me. And then one rehearsal, they kept asking me to play the same section over and over. It was alright at first, but then it became humiliating. I'm not exaggerating, must have been 40 or 50 times. They kept shouting, and at one point said 'come on, this isn't Kanye West, don't play it with swagger!'. When I finished, I felt like crying because of the humiliation, but remained professional and continued with the rehearsal. The same thing happened again the next week. This person, the person in power, never behaved like this with anyone else. They kept commenting to people that I 'mustn't be used to playing Brahms'. I took it to tribunal.

Jayne's story shocked me, and It begs the question- have there been other victims of this kind of bullying and discrimination? Maybe you know someone who has experienced something similar? Maybe you're a musician who has been through something like this because of the colour of your skin, your gender, background..?

I read an article recently about Nicki Minaj. The fact that her album and videos had been incredibly successful, breaking records for views, nominated for Grammys etc but that she didn't get nominated for best female or album. White female artists who were nominated for the same categories won. Nicki Minaj is famous for her body, shamelessly and proudly showing her flesh, is that what we're used to from black female artists? What happens when these artists feel they must live up to a certain image to be seen and heard? Are they able to be themselves? Are they stuck in a stereotype?

Eluxe magazine published an article in March 2016 about female sexualisation in pop called 'expressive or exploited?'

Within the article, they explored the issue and talked about many artists such as Britney Spears and Miley Cyrus, but the article begins by discussing the Black Panther Movement and how Chaka Khan was a member of it. The writer points out that Chaka didn't wear provocative military outfits, but instead traditional African outfits, or the black leather jacket, polo neck and beret which characterised the movement. The writer states that the sexualisation of black women in music is 'female empowerment designed by men' which really struck me.

We could argue that until society changes it's view on mental health and race that the music industry will not either. But as we've discussed in other chapters, perhaps the music industry ahead of the game when it comes to acceptance compared to other industries?

I'm hoping that this has shed light on some of the issues within mental health, the music industry and race and made people think about how the music industry has been functioning when it comes to race.

SELF-CARE AND GUIDANCE

If you are feeling depressed and anxious because of discrimination, abuse, victimisation, any of the organizations listed at the back would love to hear from you to provide emotional support.

- Citizens advice can offer help and guidance on race discrimination if you feel you have been a victim of this and would like practical support. CitizensAdvice.org.uk can advise on who to contact in your area.

- If, like Jayne, you have experienced bullying and discrimination because of your race, some law firms specialise in Race Discrimination and may be a good starting point if you are thinking of legal action.

12. Sexuality

12. Sexuality

When I think about sexuality in the music industry, I think of Prince. So sexually explicit in his lyrics, his music, and his image. There may be issues within sexuality and mental health for some musicians. Why did Prince have such a pre-occupation with sex? It would have been so interesting to talk to Prince to find this out, I am a massive Prince fan.

The music industry is so sexualised, it's become common place to see young bikini clad women shaking their wares in front of the camera whilst sucking a lolly pop. For some female artists to wear bras and knickers on stage, to imitate sex, to straddle a large ball and swing through the air. I feel that this alone would be enough to fill a book, but alas, I haven't been able to get hold of Miley Cyrus. What has this done to the mental health of the artists, musicians and indeed the dancers who have been involved in the music videos and on tour? Some may say it's been empowering, to be seen in such a way, to be seen at all. Others may say it's been degrading, but that they accept that this is what the industry wants, what the fans want and they tolerate it as exploitation. Some may not be bothered by it at all. Beyonce has opened up frequently about how she and other female artists are not being manipulated, and it is their choice to show their bodies to be seen as sexual entities and not make apologies for it.

In 2014, Gina Prince-Bythwood film was released: 'Beyond The Lights' about Noni Jean and her struggles as a female singer who is new to the music industry. Many women have been in this position; feeling fortunate, not wanting opportunities to slip away, perhaps in this scenario, a woman in the industry could feel manipulated?

There are male artists who have famously posed wearing very little clothing in the name of music such as Tupac, Marky Mark, D'Angelo, Justin Bieber and many,

many more.

We've talked about gender, we've talked about image. Both of those contribute towards sexuality in the music industry. It's rare that you see men in the background of music videos wearing speedos and dancing around. Seeing women sexualised in this way is the norm and it's damaging to young people who are seeing this on a daily basis. I spoke to one of the parents I see regularly and asked her to make a comment about this for the book:

I don't want my daughter to see it. She's 8. I think she should be playing with My Little Ponies and swinging on the swings at the park. We don't show that kind of thing to her, but she sees it at friend's houses or catches it on CBBC, they have programs about the charts and show music videos on there. If I see a Little Mix video on there, I immediately want to run over and cover her eyes and say 'that's not how women have to be you know. You don't have to show your body or be anyone's girlfriend if you don't want to be. It scares me, what's in store for them but in relation to what you're doing, I do think that the music industry does need to take responsibility. These artists are role models, they are no matter what they say or try to get out of. It's not right to show children that this is how you should dress, look and act.

It's important to address the issues around sexual orientation in relation to the music industry. I feel it's been well documented that over the years, certain artist have had to keep their homosexuality under wraps. I remember rumours in the 90's that a certain member of a boy band was gay. When he finally did come out, he said he was 'strongly advised' not to come out to the public as the fans who bought his music would be disappointed and this would lead to a backlash. Other artists such as Will Young had reportedly been through a hard time immediately after winning Pop Idol, being determined not to keep his homosexuality a secret. And why should he? Would a heterosexual musician be told to keep their heterosexuality under wraps for the sake of the fans?

George Michael

When I was thinking about sexuality in the music industry and how that relates to mental health, George Michael was the first person I thought of. I remember seeing an interview with him when I was in my teens talking about how pressures of being a star had made it difficult to come out, and that there had actually been strong suggestions from the people he worked with that he keep his sexuality a secret. He admitted that he had been out to family and friends since he was 19. The stigma around AIDS and misunderstandings of what that meant made it even harder to come out.

It was only when he was caught having sex in a public bathroom in California that the world did have confirmation that George Michael was gay. He was arrested, it was massively publicized and could have been the end of his career. But George turned it into an opportunity. He said in an interview with The Independent in 2016 that committing the illegal act in that men's bathroom was a subconsciously deliberate act, driven by the longing to be allowed to be himself and live a life, that up until then had felt 'fraudulent'. He released a controversial, tongue in cheek video to the single 'Outside' which was written about the incident and which went on to sell hundreds and thousands of copies.

The people who had advised George Michael to keep his sexuality a secret could surely only have been doing it for personal gain? The hint that he might not like females sexually may have been the end of his career, or so they thought. What a strange and torturous way of thinking this is, and how ridiculously ignorant.

George spoke about traumas from childhood in an interview with The Mirror, citing that suicides of his uncle and Grandfather had always haunted him and he worried that depression ran in the family. He stated that within the space of 3 years from 1994 onwards, he had lost his partner and his mother. These significant deaths caused him to spiral into depression and at times he said he had indeed felt suicidal.

There were rumours around 2015 that George had become a recluse and wasn't leaving his house at all. He had apparently ended a 15 year relationship and had also been involved in an accident recently to this. By all accounts, he had become addicted to prescription drugs which had made it difficult for him to function and had led him to have little self esteem surrounding his image and music. A battle with pneumonia left him unable to complete his most recent tour in Australia and issued he this statement:

"I have tried in vain to work my way through the trauma that the doctors who saved my life warned me I would experience. They recommended complete rest and the type of post-traumatic counselling which is available in cases like mine but I'm afraid I believed (wrongly) that making music and getting out there to perform for the audiences that bring me such joy would be therapy enough in itself. Unfortunately, I seriously underestimated how difficult this year would be."

Friends of George Michael said that before his death, he was planning a new album and that music was his 'sanctuary'.

In the chapter on Image, a transgender musician has allowed me to feature part of a session we had together. I spoke to Sara who is another transgender musician met who approached me when she heard I was writing this book. Sara's issues are more around her sexuality and specifically the problems she has when trying to start a sexual relationship with people and her experiences of this within the music industry:

It wouldn't be very helpful if I started talking about this without giving you a brief outline of me and what I'm about. I'm transgender. I started life as a boy, then a man. When I was 26, roughly 15 years ago, I decided that I'd had enough of lying to myself and everyone around me and that I'd try, hard though it was going to be, to be true to who I was. I'd always felt different. I'd always wondered if I was just a 'girly' boy and would grow into liking football, and trains and girls but it never happened. I like girls, don't get me wrong, but I'm not sexually attracted to them. I love the way they look, smell, dress, wear their hair, hell, I am a girl! I have no desire to sleep with them. I've had relationships with girls. That's something that I feel guilty about now and I've had the chance to apologise to some of those beautiful women who have helped me shape who I am. I knew it wasn't right, but my longing to fit in and have my family stop asking me why I haven't a girlfriend overcame everything else. Somewhere along the way, I started playing the piano and discovered I had quite a nice singing voice too. It was odd for people though, because my singing voice is fortunately quite feminine and so it fits with how I look now. I sing mainly ballads, quite dark, but I like to think they're easy to listen to, they have pleasant melodies, my piano playing is competent.

Now I'm a woman in the music industry, I find that people behave differently towards me. I am feminine looking, I am pretty. Men do come onto me, I do gig a lot and this happens frequently. I get it. They see me on stage, I wear glamorous outfits and do my hair and make up and they want to talk to me, they're interested. They hear me singing about love and darkness and they want to know more. I am attracted to men. I always have been. My first relationship with a man was someone I'd met who worked in the music industry. He'd seen me perform, bought me a drink. He was really sweet and open and I remember thinking how refreshing it was that he wasn't creepy. He wasn't trying to sign me or ask what he could do for me as others have done in the past. We lasted for 6 months. It was wonderful. He didn't mind that I was transgender, he liked it in fact. We broke up because it become clear that although I thought we were serious, and he seemed to think we were serious, he wanted to keep our relationship a secret. He kept saying he needed time and to 'process' and think about what he was going to say to people. I didn't understand, did he think people would be able to tell as soon as they met me? That he would be shamed? He didn't know when he met me, he was shocked, but it was a nice shocked, like when you find a suitcase abandoned in the road and find £1,000 in it (I can imagine). I was so disappointed but I pretended that I understood. I hated him deep down and I think I still do.

The second relationship I had with a man was with a member of the band I was in. I played keys and did some backing vocals. When we got publicity shots done, I was always in the centre being the only 'girl'. I was glamorous and good looking, the rest of the band, all male, would stand around me looking serious. When I saw the pictures afterwards, I liked how they looked but for the first time, it struck me how women are treated in this industry. What would it have been like if I'd have been an unattractive woman wearing dungarees and my hair a mess? I don't think that would have been OK, do you? My boyfriend was the drummer and everyone knew he was my boyfriend. I loved that, I loved saying it, I loved holding his hand walking down the street, I especially liked him calling me his 'girlfriend'. The first time I heard that was truly one of the best experiences of my life. He also knew I was trans early on, it was a relief to tell him and after my first experience with a man, I was apprehensive. Yes, he'd accepted me at first but his reluctance to tell people suggested that he didn't and that he was confused by the whole thing. This one was different in that he wanted people to know, but after a while, it was me who was the problem. I started doubting his judgement, questioning his motives. Why was he with me? Was there something wrong with him? Why did he want me? I realized at that point that I had a lot of demons around self esteem, self worth and who I was. It was all too much too soon. I broke his heart, it was not a good time. I am so sorry. I wasn't ready and I didn't know who I was.

In 2015, I was on stage in Paris and a beautiful man was sitting in the audience. He kept smiling at me and closing his eyes when I sang. I was trying not to be distracted, but I couldn't help it! Afterwards, he found me at the door of the green room and said in the most wonderful accent 'you are stunning and your voice is breathtaking' it was like something from a film. We've been married for 2 years now. I know that I still have things I need to work through but I'm feeling less confused and more in touch with who I am than ever before.

We see here with Sara that she is in a place mentally where she feels able to acknowledge that she still has issues around her sexuality within the music industry but that she admits to being more comfortable with who she is.

David Bowie was known for his androgynous look early on, people were confused as to whether he was male or female. The same could be said for singers such as Boy George and Pete Burns. This androgynous look influenced many artists and paved the way for people like Grace Jones, Annie Lennox and more recent singer Le Roux.

We, as an audience have been presented with these images for a long time, maybe it's less shocking than it was when Bowie first came on the scene.

With regards to these musicians and others we've discussed in this chapter, the music industry may be the platform to express individuality, that freedom of expression is wholly accepted and embraced. However, we do need to also acknowledge that not everyone has this open-minded acceptance in music, where artists are still being told that they must keep their sexuality under wraps. Let's support those artists and keep talking about these issues, raising awareness and providing encouragement.

SELF-CARE AND GUIDANCE

- If you are feeling in any way exploited, bullied or discriminated against with regards to your sexual identity, there is information at the end of this book on who you may want to contact.

- We have come a long way in how we see diversity, but there's still a long way to go. Of course it's wonderful for musicians to be themselves and show the world who they are, but those people need to be ready for that and not feel pressured.

13. Pressure and Stress

Stress is a colossal issue. It effects everyone to different extremes and can be a catalyst for mental and physical health problems.

The stresses within the music industry can be immense and do not just effect musicians, but industry workers in different roles and for varied reasons. Major record labels receive pressure from executives to find and release new material that is going to make money. They may have criteria to fill, a certain image, a certain sound. They may also have been given a deadline to find an act and their job may be on the line due to whether they find this one or not. There is pressure from all sides, and once the artist has become involved, they too feel the pressure of the expectations that have been placed on them to live up to what everyone had hoped for. There are people who own rehearsal rooms or recording studios who experience stress due to their business, roles and the people within the music industry who they deal with. They may have bands coming in who cause them stress, money issues, pressures to provide a service on demand.

There's definitely pressure to be confident if you're making your way in the music industry, especially if you're starting out. I work with music students who are regularly told that as well as having talent, they need to 'sell themselves' and 'stand out from the crowd'. I was approached by a few different people after a talk I did at a conference saying that they had been told to schmooze and network but they really find it hard to talk to people. They have faith in their talent but they wish that their chances of 'making it' in the industry didn't depend on their ability to socialise. I told each of the musicians that there is some truth to the networking, but that it didn't have to be all down to how well they can sell themselves, although this is an element. There is an expectation if people really want something, they will do what needs to be done, especially in such a competitive industry. This lifestyle cultivates anxiety especially within people who find it hard to meet up to those expectations.

Something else I've heard from musicians on a number of occasions, no matter what the discipline, is that they have it drummed into them that if they have any spare time whatsoever, they are doing something wrong. One of the people who said this is, worryingly, a well known figure in the music industry who is regularly talking to young and vulnerable people hoping for a career in music. What effect does this have on people's mental health? To constantly be on edge, and lamenting on what more can be done? What more do I have to do?

The music industry workers also feel pressure from fans and the audiences who are buying the music of the artists they have signed. If they have an artist on their roster who has previously released a number 1 album, there are obviously expectations that this same artist will make even more with the second release. Obviously, from this, there is a massive pressure for the artist to 'do better' to reinvent themselves perhaps, and to do something exciting, or even just release the same music to please existing fans.

So much stress is rife in all sectors. I worked with a client who worked in artist & repertoire at a relatively large record label. A&R are responsible for scouting new talent and developing the talent so they're 'industry ready' for release. It is a difficult but highly enjoyable job when the person in question feels they have achieved their goal and found 'the next big thing':

> *Last year, I discovered the most amazing artist. He was incredible. He was singing and playing the guitar at an open mic night. It wasn't even that his voice was that great, or his guitar playing. It was his lyrics and performance. His songs were stunning. He was the real deal, he was something new and special and I just knew.*
>
> It sounds like you get a lot out of finding new talent.
>
> *Most definitely. I love music. You must love music to be able to do this. I know people in A&R who stopped listening to music and said they were getting bored and that the just wanted to chill and not listen to any music when they got home. A few weeks later, they'd quit. There was always a pattern, I've started seeing it more and more. I love my job, but it is hard.*
>
> You originally contacted me because you were feeling stressed?
>
> *Yes, I do feel stressed, there's a lot of pressure in the job. And it doesn't end when I leave the office, because I'm always on the lookout. You could say I was always*

'on edge' but that simplifies it a bit to be honest. Most people walk past someone busking and hear a few seconds of the song, but I stop and watch and listen. I've scouted buskers in the past. Sometimes they've been signed, sometimes not, but they're golden, shining stars, and you can bet they have a story.

So, you feel you're always on edge. That sounds tiring.

It is, it's exciting and tiring and I find it really hard to switch off. I have things that I like to do, I think 'when I get home, I'll watch this, or call this person for a chat' and more often than not, I'm out of the door going to a gig. I have a brilliant social life, but not with the people I want to be or should be socialising with. There have been times recently where I've been told there are other people who would take my job in a second and I need to remember that I'm lucky. My manager pulled me in last week to say she wanted me to find someone 'stellar' to support a world class act on tour and it had to be someone new and fresh. I've heard that so many times, but I did panic. I know my job is in demand, I know I'm lucky, but what if I don't find this person? This artist? I can't sleep now because it's just going over and over in my head. I was actually thinking of cancelling this session, so I'd have more time to look for the artist.

It sounds like the boundaries are blurred for you. You're intending to have time to yourself when you leave work, but actually you're working all the time, and then thinking about work when you're supposed to be switching off. There's also something there about putting your job before your own health.

Yeah, that's it. How are you supposed to find someone when you're knackered all the time and need to sleep? I love what I do, but sometimes I wonder how long I can do this for without exploding.

Define 'exploding'.

A breakdown. I've been there before. About seven years ago. It was just too much. I wasn't A&R then, but I did have a high-pressured job, an assistant to a manager. He expected stuff of me professionally that I just wasn't going to do. It was like 'The Devil Wears Prada'. He was calling me at 2am telling me I had to get down to some club and help him with a comatose guitarist and try and book him a place at rehab immediately. It was stuff like that every week. It was exhausting. I learnt a lot, but I hated it by the end. People think the music industry is glamorous. It can be, but behind all of that, there's a lot of shit that happens to make it all work. I don't want to be part of the shit. That's why I quit working for him. I'm afraid the same thing is going to happen again. I'm burning myself out.

> We discussed the client's burn out and what's driving her to make these decisions, the stress she feels directly from management and the industry that she has chosen to work in.
>
> *It's hard just to remind myself that this is a job and I can choose to leave whenever I want. I'm a woman, I've worked hard to be where I am, and I want to keep going. You have to go all or nothing with this industry, you really do. There have been so many casualties, some many people I know and respect who have not been able to hack it. I want to keep going.*

In a manner of speaking, this client had started to burn out already, but she had recognised her situation, she was self-aware and knew where she was heading if she carried on the way she was.

The client wanted to continue in A&R, but she knew what she'd had to do to get where she was and was reluctant to give up, even if her mental health was at risk. We talked about self-care, making sure that the time she had away from work was her night. Would her job really suffer as much as she suspected if she went to eight gigs a week instead of twelve? Giving herself that one night may be the key to not unravelling and being able to carry on living the life she said she 'loved'.

There is a question about stress and how you handle it if it is part your job. How can stress be your job? Ask someone with a high-pressured music industry job. The rewards are there, but stress is par for the course. I talked to a label owner a while ago who laughed once asked 'why don't you take a break? A weekend away?' His reply was to laugh and say, 'you're kidding, aren't you?' To him, the idea of a break was preposterous. He recognised he was stressed, but not willing or able to make a change and do something about it in order to reduce his anxiety.

For many people in the music industry, their office is a tour bus, backstage at a gig or in a recording studio. The level of pressure and stress is very high compared to other industries. As discussed earlier, the line between a social life and work is very narrow. For the client who we looked at earlier in the chapter, going to a gig could have been veiled as a social occasion, but to her, it was work. How do you manage that?

Music producers, mixers and engineers live an unusual existence. They work on projects, albums, EP's or music for films and spend long periods of time in isolation, trying to get things finished and get the right sound and the right mix. I interviewed a music producer recently who had worked on some prolific albums:

> *Well, you've asked me how I handle stress, and to be honest, I don't know if*

I do handle it! My wife would say I don't for sure. She's told me so many times 'do what makes you happy', this does make me happy, but it does really stress me out sometimes. I'd say, when I can see that I'm heading into a difficult place and in danger of getting proper stressed, when there's a lot of pressure on, I get up and walk away for an hour. I walk about outside, go and get a coffee, come back slightly more refreshed and ready to carry on. I mean, my wife would tell you, there are times when I will literally spend 4 days straight in the recording studio.

That's a long time, do you eat? Sleep? How does that work?

Well, as you can see, I've got a little sofa there and a fridge. I keep myself in water and food so I'm good. It's turning off that's difficult, I've got to wind down which really isn't easy. I have to have complete sensory deprivation, no music, no tv, maybe I'll read a magazine, then I call my wife and go to sleep. Thank god we don't have kids, I'd never see them.

So, during these sessions, I could imagine day and night blur into one?

*Yeah, there are no windows and I obviously have the time on my phone, but once I'm in the studio, I don't really keep track of things. I could be working until 4 in the morning and not realize, then I think 'S***' I really need to take a break! It works for me though, in a lot of ways. There have been times where I've been close to quitting because I didn't think I'd be able to go through a period like that again*

Can you give an example?

OK, I had a big project, a band in, they must have spent about 8 weeks recording their album, then I obviously carried on in the studio long after they'd finished. There was a deadline, a lot of pressure from the record label. I knew them quite well at the label, so they were sort of passive-aggressively checking up on me, you know?! Like 'Err, when do you think you'll be finished because there are a lot of people waiting for this. Ha-ha, OK, you let us know if there's anything you need' They were calling every day, no joke. I was getting headaches but powering through. I was working 20-hour shifts, knowing that they'd call in a couple of hours and I'd want to have something to tell them. I met the deadline, I always do but it's at the detriment of my health sometimes.

What did you do once that project was over?

*I f***** slept! Saw my wife, made it up to her, took her away. Crazy life I lead!*

Stress comes in many different forms within the music industry. Sophie who co-manages a venue in Manchester which is famous for its band nights wrote this piece:

I love music, but it would be wrong and untruthful to say that I found working in music easy. Things have changed a lot over the past few years and I don't know where things are headed now. We've always put on band nights here, having 5-6 bands on each night. Once a week we have a club night which are popular too. The bands we have on play everything from folk to heavy metal. The people that work here tell me they love their jobs and that a lot of it is to do with the people, but also just being exposed to music all the time.

An average day for me would be to open up, check the venue and see what kind of state it's in. Check deliveries have been made, the place has been cleaned, everything works how it should, bar is clean and ready to go. All the equipment is backstage, tidy, in working order and that the bands who are booked in to come haven't called or cancelled, that none of the staff or off sick and if they are try and get replacements. When soundchecks are due, I mostly like to be there. If there are any problems with the bands or someone hasn't turned up, we sometimes try and replace them depending on how many we're expecting so I'll look into that. Sometimes there's problems with the bar and drinks and stuff, I help with that. Have you ever worked on a bar on a busy night? It's killer.

*I know what it's like to suffer with mental health problems. I've always had depression on and off, and stress does really affect me. My employees come to me because they know I care and they know they can talk to me about whatever's bothering them. Our sound engineer was suffering badly at one point, he was suicidal. I took him to A&E myself. I said, 'you're not doing this on my watch'. He got better for a while and then he did try and kill himself. It was horrible, I felt there must have been something I missed, and I should have stopped him. He's OK now, this was last year. I ask him all the time if he' OK, he probably gets really p****d off with me, but I don't care because I want him to know I'm here.*

Dealing with the bands themselves can be stressful. Most of the bands are really cool, but sometimes you get one that are a nightmare to deal with. They can be demanding, picking on everything, saying the venues crap, telling us we should be providing this or that. I'm always running around trying to sort things, that isn't always my job, but I do it because I don't want anyone else to be stressed either. We get blamed by bands if people don't turn up to their gigs. They don't understand that it's the promoters that are responsible for that, and some of the responsibility falls on them too for not promoting as much as they could on social media. There's a lot of pressure in music, a lot of stress. I don't know what I'd do if I didn't do this, but sometimes I wonder what it would be like to be out! I'd miss it too much.

I asked if the sound engineer would like to comment on his mental health struggles, he declined:

Maybe one day, I feel I want to talk about that and let other people hear about it but right now I'm just getting to grips with what I am going through and what it means for my life, my future, my work.

It's staggering, the amount of people I've come across whilst writing this book who suffer with their mental health, or know others in the music industry who do. Some want to talk about it, other don't. Some don't mind talking about it but don't want to be named. All OK, all completely understandable.

Again, if we can just raise awareness by talking about it, perhaps we can reduce the amount of people suffering with mental health issues within the music industry, or at least provide them with a platform where they can share. Does it mean something that people with depression and anxiety and other issues have a non-judgemental place where they can go and talk about whatever they need to talk about? As a counsellor, of course I do believe that, but I know there will be people that don't. However, even if that is your way of thinking, there's no doubt that reducing stress and pressure can do us all good, physically and mentally.

SELF-CARE AND GUIDANCE

- Managing stress is something that most people must do at some point in order to get through their day. If you're feeling stressed, try and find some time at the end of the day to think about why you've been so stressed and what can change in order to manage this. If you carry on feeling stressed and not addressing it, this could lead to further issues.

- Making small changes can make a massive impact on how you cope with stress. Sometimes, what's happening to make you stressed doesn't warrant the impact it's having on you.

- Ask yourself: is it the event that's stressful or my reaction to it? Make the choice not to be stressed and instead assess what can be done to change the situation.

- If stress is a recurring issue that is affecting your mental health and you don't feel you can manage it, it might be something that you need to talk to someone about. It's easy and cruel to say 'if you don't want to do it, someone else will' but it's also discrimination and shouldn't be tolerated. There are organisations at the back of this book who can provide help with any issues related to bullying and discrimination in the workplace.

14. Being a woman in a man's world

14. Being a woman in a man's world

We're here to talk about mental health in the music industry. I've researched a lot and spoken to many musicians and people in the industry; but I feel it wouldn't be right if I didn't look further into some of the causes of other issues and explain why they effect mental health.

I have been through certain situations in the music industry that have made me question whether these things would have happened if I had been a man. I've concluded that no, they wouldn't have. I've also questioned whether these situations were my fault and whether I 'put something out there' that meant I am treated in a certain way. With recent events in the news around gender and power in the film industry, I want to open a dialogue about these same issues within the music industry and start a conversation about other people's experiences.

I'm writing as a woman, but I'm also writing from the perspective of someone who is under represented in most industries, who doesn't hold power as men do and who must work harder to be noticed, taken seriously and acknowledged as a musician.

In this chapter around gender, it might be more difficult to read between the lines. People have come out talking about gender in the music industry. Some women may have said it was hard to be a woman; that they've worked harder to be taken seriously, not just to be viewed as an attractive woman, be objectified and given a chance based mostly on appearance.

Within this, it's important to first address the gender imbalance within the industry and within other roles, not just those of musicians and artists. Within a survey taken out by UKMusic, it was found that women make up most of the music industry work force with 60% of interns being women, 59% at entry level business positions but only 30% of senior positions. I spoke on a panel in 2017 about the future of women in the music industry. Issues came up from both the panel and the audience around why this is. Are women afraid to go for these roles, already taught that there's no point? Are women afraid to stand up and be noticed at risk of being called 'bossy' 'cocky' or worse? There was also discussion about women who are in senior positions in the music industry not helping or supporting other women.

I spoke with Martha who was an intern with a large record label between 1996-1997. Martha had enjoyed her time as an intern, but said it really shocked her how she was viewed by others and treated by the only female executive whom she approached one day:

> *I really wanted to talk to her. I kept thinking 'what's the point in having this opportunity if I don't try and talk to a woman who is where I want to be one day?'. I emailed her and didn't receive a reply. Someone else suggested just waiting a bit longer and seeing if an opportunity came up to see her. About 6 months later, she happened to be sitting in on a meeting I was involved in and I approached her afterwards. I told her what an influence she had been on my decision making and that she was an inspiration. I asked her if she had any advice for me on my future and what was the best route to take . She barely looked at me and then said, 'it's not likely you'll get a senior role in this company, but good luck to you'. She walked away, and I felt awful. I questioned everything I was doing. I know it sounds silly, but I just felt really low and worthless for a couple of weeks. Her words had really got to me and I was just depressed for like, 3 weeks. I got over it and carried on. I did do well, but I discovered that the company wasn't for me and I moved on.*

This situation and the lack of support and encouragement had led Martha to question her worth, her decisions and her future. Would she have had this response if she had been male? I'm interested in why this executive said what she said, and what experiences had led her to that comment. Getting to where she was may have been difficult and she had become jaded by the process. We can only imagine what was going on for her.

3 different relationships over the past 18 years reflect my own experiences in the music industry and have really affected me. I think about the men involved from time to time. I do question what happened, how things may have turned out different if I'd 'complied'. In short, I would have been more successful if I'd been submissive. Part of me wanted to document the relationships in this book. I re-wrote the section several times before deciding to leave them out. I realised that the need to do it was more to

do with me getting some kind of relief and vindication from it. Those men know who they are, they may feel some kind of regret about how they treated me, and I hope they've thought about how they treat women in the future.

Laura Mvula

Laura Mvula is something of a recent addition to the music industry. She's been nominated for, and won MOBO, Brit and Ivor Novello awards. Her first album was released 6 years ago, and she's gone from strength to strength. However, Laura has been open in the press around her struggles with depression and anxiety. In a 2016 interview with The Guardian, she talked about her feelings around her mental health issues:

" I suffer from depression and anxiety and, in all seriousness, I would not be here today without my brother and sister's unconditional love. It still makes me wince to see my name written next to the words "mental illness", but the practical, real depth of consistent care and concern has cushioned my burden. Sometimes when I've not felt able to cry, they cry with me or for me. Or when I'm not able to ask by myself, they'll do it for me. The hardest thing has been looking my family in the eye and seeing them see me suffer and feel helpless, and it not being something that they can just fix. I know that whatever happens to me I'm not judged by them. To them I'm precious Laura, with or without the anxiety, with or without the music."

Laura Mvula's 2016 documentary for Radio 4's Women's Hour 'Generation Anxiety', looks at her own struggle with depression and anxiety whilst living in the public eye. According to recent statistics from Cambridge university, women are twice as likely to suffer from anxiety as men. There could be many reasons for this, different pressures, different expectations, gender roles etc. Or, it could be that men are less likely to open up about these issues and be honest about their anxiety.

Laura states that she feels is someone opened her up, they would see that something is really wrong. Laura talks extremely candidly about her anxiety, being on the tube, being alone, fears around many things. She talks about her fear of being alone and specifically how difficult this is being on the road as a musician, having to explain to people that she needs someone with her when she's sleeping and even going into the toilet. In one point, Laura talks about a panic attack that she had at Glastonbury:

"I had a panic attack one time at Glastonbury. I remember looking down at the keyboard and being like 'is there a way to disguise this? 'cos this could be it. It's one thing to be around friends and family and it's another for the world to see it. Any moment you're going to be seen and you're going to be put into a mental institution and there's nothing you can do about it'. That's a fear."

What Laura is doing here is so important. Not only is she raising awareness of these issues, but she's also allowing herself to be seen as vulnerable and exposing her mental health issues, something that not many musicians would want to do.

Heidi Dewhurst, a singer songwriter based in Manchester mentioned on my radio show that she had put together a collective of female singer songwriters to perform at gigs across Manchester. I was curious as to why she had decided to do this and what opportunities she felt she wanted to create for women in music:

I started the collective on somewhat of a whim back in January 2016. Ever since I was a child the idea of having a club or a gang always appealed and suddenly, all the way into my adulthood I found myself with the ability to make something happen- I could realise this dream, and on a big scale! The idea initially was to get all (or as many as I could) the girls that I'd become friends with within the Manchester music scene, and put on a gig, the ultimate girl's night, if you will. It was always intended for anybody and everybody to be welcomed into the audience, but I wanted to have an all female line up. It occurred to me, as it has to everyone, that at your average open mic night the performers were 99% male, and whilst that is brilliant (seriously, our Manchester lads have some talent!) I think we all agree that it would be great if the line ups were a little more diverse, which I'm noticing is happening more and more as time goes by, partly thanks to many dear friends of mine including the awesome The Northern Rambler and Bread Records- shout out to you guys, who follow a similar agenda to myself. I also have Charlotte H Lawrence working with me on the social media side of things to keep the collective going strong. The god(esses!) smiled on us and our first event went down a storm, and now somehow here we are two years later with half of Manchester (or so it feels) on a hype for whatever we come up with next from month to month.

There does seem to be a re-addressing of gender equality in lots of different industries, some of this is being highly publicized in the media. But why is there such a mis-match of the kinds of roles that women are in within the music industry? Are women not encouraged in the same way? Are they not expected to fill these jobs?

Recording Engineer, mixer and music producer Marta Salogni wrote this following piece. I asked her about mental health in the music industry and specifically the lack of role models she had around the type of work she wanted to do as a woman in the industry:

I believe mental health is one of the most underestimated and affected aspects of a job in the Music Industry and it touches all its sectors.

A field which in most cases success is volatile, the necessity of exceeding expectations often without even knowing what they are, precarious financial security yet the need of investing all available time and resources into a career which promises no reliable longevity.

Working in this field often requires confronting with challenges, both personally and professionally. The aftermath of our decisions not only affect ourselves, but the people close to us - families, partners, friends.

Comfort zones are frequently pushed and a solid capacity to quickly adapt is required. All of this, whilst demonstrating to hold control over whichever situation is being presented or has just unfolded.

My path as a music professional has taken me through different levels of its structure, in which I both recognised, experienced, and tried to improve those elements described above.

The added factor of being a woman, part of the staggering minority in the industry, has fuelled my desire to progress and a sense of duty towards wanting to fix the lack of representation in the field.

I started to perceive a possible failure not only as a personal defeat, but as a wider responsibility.

At the very start, because of the lack of exposure (rather than the mere lack) of non-male role models, I was made feel that my perceived gender could have determined an obstacle to my success.

I use the words 'made feel' and 'perceived' because I personally do not believe in gender myself, but I rather see it yet another social construct and constraint. What I believe in is the factual struggle of the minority and the consequent lack of diversity in the field.

When I looked around me, as a teenager, I couldn't find anybody 'like me', who was doing 'what I wanted to do'.

Especially in those formative years, when the desire for identity is at its peak, I felt both scared and excited to be challenging the status-quo, and to be setting a precedent for other people 'like me', who in the future would have known they are not alone and their vision is not an illusion.

Mine is the fascination with manipulating sound through mechanical mediums.

I have always seen a beautiful conceptual meaning in that, a poetry which drives me today still. The bare monetary side of the job, the excesses of the 1980's or whichever fairy tale some like to tell, has never interested me but rather annoyed me, as if they tinted a sacred art with a colour that doesn't belong to it.

Through my personal and professional growth, I finally met other like-minded individuals with whom I feel we created a community, which became a driving force behind a long-awaited, powerful moment of change in the history of the Music Industry - redefining its core, to represent a more inclusive, essentially diverse, fairer and unbiased reality. I believe such an improvement can only reflect positively on many aspects that affect mental health in the field, and I hope it can provide support, build the bridges that fortify its otherwise feeble and unreliable structure.

I'm so grateful to Marta for sharing that and raising awareness of an issue that is gaining ground but still needs a lot of people to sit up and take notice. I was asked to speak at a conference called We Are Robots. The panel was 'The Future of Women in The Music Industry'. That's where I met Marta, and I found the whole panel extremely empowering. Strong, intelligent women who had fought to be where they were. Each of us had experiences of some kind of mental health struggle and had had to work hard to be where they were.

Lady Gaga

I remembered seeing a video that people had shared of Prince William and Lady Gaga having an open conversation with one another over skype about mental health. My first thoughts without even watching it was that it was a wonderful thing to do. I was really impressed with Prince William, Kate Middleton and Prince Harry for starting their Heads Together campaign for raising awareness of mental health issues.

I started looking into Lady Gaga after this, primarily to talk about on the radio show, but also because I was really intrigued by her willingness to be so open about mental health. Since then, she's shared a lot more and spoken candidly about her struggled with post-traumatic stress disorder due to rape she experienced at the age of 19. She published an open letter in December 2016. I read this on my show, and I'm publishing it in this book because I think it's fantastic and will genuinely help others. I love that she has stated that she's a powerful woman, but that even powerful women experience vulnerability and periods where they find it hard to cope. Here's the letter:

'I have wrestled for some time about when, how and if I should reveal my diagnosis of Post-Traumatic Stress Disorder (PTSD). After five years of searching for the answers to my chronic pain and the change I have felt in my brain, I am finally well enough to tell you. There is a lot of shame attached to mental illness, but it's important that you know that there is hope and a chance for recovery.

It is a daily effort for me, even during this album cycle, to regulate my nervous system so that I don't panic over circumstances that to many would seem like normal life situations. Examples are leaving the house or being touched by strangers who simply want to share their enthusiasm for my music.

I also struggle with triggers from the memories I carry from my feelings of past years on tour when my needs and requests for balance were being ignored. I was overworked and not taken seriously when I shared my pain and concern that something was wrong. I ultimately ended up injured on the Born This Way Ball. That moment and the memory of it has changed my life forever. The experience of performing night after night in mental and physical pain ingrained in me a trauma that I relive when I see or hear things that remind me of those days.

I also experience something called dissociation which means that my mind doesn't want to relive the pain so "I look off and I stare" in a glazed over state. As my doctors have taught me, I cannot express my feelings because my pre-frontal cortex (the part of the brain that controls logical, orderly thought) is overridden by the amygdala (which stores emotional memory) and sends me into a fight or flight response. My body is in one place and my mind in another. It's like the panic accelerator in my mind gets stuck and I am paralyzed with fear.

When this happens, I can't talk. When this happens repeatedly, it makes me have a common PTSD reaction which is that I feel depressed and unable to function like I used to. It's harder to do my job. It's harder to do simple things like take a shower. Everything has become harder. Additionally, when I am unable to regulate my anxiety, it can result in somatization, which is pain in the body caused by an inability to express my emotional pain in words.

But I am a strong and powerful woman who is aware of the love I have around me from my team, my family and friends, my doctors and from my incredible fans who I know will never give up on me. I will never give up on my dreams of art and music. I am continuing to learn how to transcend this because I know I can. If you relate to what I am sharing, please know that you can too.

Traditionally, many associate PTSD as a condition faced by brave men and women that serve countries all over the world. While this is true, I seek to raise awareness that this mental illness affects all kinds of people, including our youth. I pledge not only to help our youth not feel ashamed of their own conditions, but also to lend support to those servicemen and women who suffer from PTSD. No one's invisible pain should go unnoticed.

I am doing various modalities of psychotherapy and am on medicine prescribed by my psychiatrist. However, I believe that the most inexpensive and perhaps the best medicine in the world is words. Kind words... positive words... words that help people who feel ashamed of an invisible illness to overcome their shame and feel free. This is how I and we can begin to heal. I am starting today, because secrets keep you sick. And I don't want to keep this secret anymore.

A note from my psychologist, Dr Nancy;

If you think you might have PTSD, please seek professional help. There is so much hope for recovery. Many people think that the event that stimulated PTSD needs to be the focus. Yet often, people will experience the same event and have completely different reactions to it. It is my opinion that trauma occurs in an environment where your feelings and emotional experience are not valued, heard and understood. The specific event is not the cause of traumatic experience. This lack of a "relational home" for feelings is the true cause of traumatic experience. Finding support is key.

I asked Polly Paulusma to write something for this book. She had such a unique story to tell. Both men and women are affected by having a baby, but Polly talked about her struggled with post traumatic stress in relation to trying to make a living in the music industry. Here's a snippet, you can read the full version at the end of this book:

Having a baby was a terrifying gamble of economics for me; like many working would-be parents I faced the stark choice of 1) making more money than my partner, 2) making enough money to pay for some childcare, or 3) taking a pause from my music-making career. So, as I expected baby number one, I threw myself into my work; I recorded my second album at enormous expense to my small record label and committed to three 2-week tours (two in the UK, one in Italy) by the time my baby was 9 months old. What I didn't expect was post-natal depression, which I experienced during the second tour, when my baby was about 6 months old. I'd heard so many friends and family members describing their own symptoms of clinical depression, but it was an eye-opener to experience it first-hand. One morning I woke up and it was as if I had been surrounded by a milky-white mist. All tasks had suddenly become Herculean, impossible to complete. I went to a supermarket to buy some basics, and emerged blinking three hours later with nothing. Lists became tangles of confusion-web. And I was meant to be touring. The only way through it was for my husband, who had taken time off work to care for our baby while I was on stage, to take over. He organised my set lists, assembled my instrument setups, plugged together my jack leads, got my plectrums and picks organised and then literally pushed me out onto the stage. I felt like a zombie, an emptiness out there before people.

Society in general must be more aware of the mental health issues that can arise for women after having a baby. Your life changes, it's obvious that that's going to happen, but until it does, you have no clue as to how and the impact that the baby will have on absolutely everything. Maintaining your usual routine is difficult, you need lots of support. Simple things like going to the shop become a massive achievement, any mother who can manage to spend half an hour on her own during this time would count herself as fortunate. So, imagine having a job where you were on stage night after night, having to perform to an audience and portray an air that everything is all right? Polly achieved all of this and more and was aware that although she was really struggling, she had made a choice to carry on, not to take time out. In many ways, living life in the music industry can have advantages in terms of having that creative outlet, being fortunate enough to be able to get onto stage and sing your songs if that's what you want to do. It's such an expectation on mothers to 'do what's right'. Post-natal depression as a very serious mental health issue. It can have repercussions for everyone around and be the difference between a positive new born experience and an extremely negative one. It doesn't mean you're a bad parent or that you're to blame for your depression, it's something that's happening that you need help with and that's nothing to be ashamed of.

I've talked a lot in this chapter about women. I felt that all of these issues needed to be addressed. However, it would be ignorant to talk about gender in the music industry and not point out the rate at which we're losing male musicians to suicide each year. In 2017, Chester Bennington and Chris Cornell both took their lives. I talk about these artists later on in the book, but they are a prime example of how men, especially of a certain age are more likely to commit suicide. According to research by The Samaritans, the highest suicide rate in 2017 was for men aged 45-49. These statistics are talked about more and more in the media and continue to grow. Women are more likely to seek help for mental health disorders and are, according to recent research, more likely to have suicidal thoughts. However, it's no secret that there is more of a stigma for men to suffer with their mental health. For all of the reasons discussed in this book, the music industry is particularly difficult when an individual is suffering. There are certain expectations to live up to an image that is perhaps false. As discussed earlier, a person who has become a massive success is still a person, anxiety and depression does not dissipate, and in some ways develops even more intensely with pressures of a different kind. I have spoken to several male musicians who have explained that when they voiced their mental health issues to the people around them, it was met with negativity which led to shame and embarrassment. In one case, someone felt that they'd actually lost out on work due to their admission of suffering from depression. How are we supposed to battle these stigmas if 'the powers that be' are the ones who are lacking in empathy and understanding? I cannot say this enough- let's challenge people, let's speak up. Together, we really can make a difference.

SELF-CARE AND GUIDANCE

- If you are being bullied or discriminated against, harassed, abused, controlled in the music industry or any industry, it's not always easy to report, especially when there are things at stake. If you don't have support and don't have anyone to turn to, there are people you can call who are there to help.

At the end of this book there is a list of some organisations who are there to listen and support you whatever the hour.

15. How the industry can be more supportive

I spoke at a conference recently and the issue of how to deal with artists who may be suffering with their mental health came up frequently. One of the people who approached me after the event was a manager and a label owner. He very humbly admitted that it was his own experiences as a musician which inspired him to start a label that was respectful and nurturing of artists and who was aware of possible mental health issues. I found this really encouraging, but I'm also well aware that this way of thinking is not as wide spread as we would hope.

We touched upon it in the chapter about Life On Tour and the transcript of a session with Gary, the tour manager. He described a scene where he had to physically break up fights between band members. But what happens when people are struggling with their mental health? Is it your job as a manager or a part of the crew or industry professionals who come in contact with these artists to look after their mental health and wellbeing? Do you have a duty of care to take of them?

If this was any other business, there would be an HR department who could refer for counselling if an employee is suffering, there would be a chance to talk to your line manager about why you're finding it hard to keep up with your work or missed a deadline. Recently, I spoke to a friend who plays in an orchestra. They pointed out that due to the nature of an orchestra and the various positions, that if you don't get on with the person sitting next to you, there is nobody to complain to. You must spend a lot of time with this person and such issues can be all-consuming when you have to work with them every day.

Who is there to support mental health in the music industry?

Manager, producer, author and journalist Simon Napier Bell had this to say about the relationship between an artist and their manager:

Nearly all artists suffer from a permanent inner disquiet, it's not only part of being an artist, it's the thing that drives their art. Many of them have suffered some sort of childhood trauma. It could have been the death of a parent or sibling, a divorce, some sort of physical or sexual abuse, or some other type of emotional upheaval in early life. In most cases it leaves a smouldering hurt that drives their creativity.

For a manager, the nature of that trauma is irrelevant. But you can be sure, if you're managing a creative artist, sometimes in their childhood something happened that triggered their creativity. It's as if each new work they come up with is created specifically to assuage something that nags at their brain. I've never met or managed any worthwhile artist who wasn't like that.

The actual cause of that inner disquiet is no business of the manager, his job is to manage the talent that results from it not to query how it came about. Just be happy it's there and exploit it. That may sound callous but it's the reality; it's what the artist wants of his manager.

I never discuss with any artist things that touch on their personal life, nor discuss the source of their depressions or artistic moods, I just deal with them as best I can and create an infrastructure on which they can work for success. As a manager, I'm hired to exploit their talent. I'm not a psychiatrist hired to treat the source of it.

Art is a symptom of an artist's inner pain. The manager's job is to commercialise the symptom it produces and help the artist use it to build a satisfactory life.

I thought this was interesting, it also confirmed my fears around management. Simon is saying here that he and other managers are there to exploit and have little interest in supporting the artist. I'm confident there are managers who don't feel like this, and I've actually met a couple of them, but I'm concerned that there are people in the industry who think like this, who may think that the very existence of this book is ridiculous.

Music Support offer services to musicians who are suffering with their mental health. They, like Helpmusicians, offer a 24/7 helpline where they have actually put musicians into rehab. They have tents at festivals for musicians to go to if they're feeling anxious and where trained professionals are on hand to help. I realize as I write this that some people may think this is extreme, that these services are on offer to people in the music industry. I believe these services should be standard to everyone in the music industry. These services and others like them are there and all managers, industry professionals need to be aware of them for their own health and those around them.

Some artists and bands have psychologists on tour with them, especially if they are prone to depression or other issues and risk suffering whilst on tour or away from home. Again, what forward thinking this is and how wonderful for the musicians to have a therapist on call. This is not the norm but maybe we're getting there?

Chris Difford's contribution outlines the effects of fame and money at a young age, and the substance abuse he found himself embroiled in. Would it have been different if he had been able to talk to someone on a daily basis? If his record company were aware of his issues and could offer to support his problems with therapy? Would it not help all musicians to be offered these services? For managers and label executives and everyone else to be aware that someone is suffering and in order to offer their best as a musician, they need help and support. It's all too common a story to hear of artists suffering and still being pushed to tour, record and perform, until we read about them burning out and having to cancel their tour dates due to fatigue or exhaustion. I strongly believe that mental health for musicians and other music industry professionals would improve if there as an awareness and therefore knowledge and support.

Chris Cornell

Chris Cornell was the lead singer of bands 'SoundGarden' and 'Audioslave'. He was one of the world's most respected musicians and his suicide in May 2017 led to an onslaught of tributes from fans all over the world, including the biggest names in the music industry.

What makes Chris Cornell's suicide all the more tragic is that 2 months later, his close friend and godfather to his son, Chester Bennington of Linkin Park also committed suicide in the same way.

Lead singer of Pearl Jam, Eddie Vedder wrote his feelings around the time of his friend's death on the Pearl Jam message board. Here are some of the comments he made:

"About two days after the news, I think it was the second night we were sleeping in this little cabin near the water, a place he would've loved. And all these memories started coming in about 1:30am like woke me up. Like big memories, memories I would think about all the time. Like the memories were big muscles.

And then I couldn't stop the memories. And trying to sleep it was like if the neighbours had the music playing and you couldn't stop it. But then it was fine because then it got into little memories. It just kept going and going and going. And I realized how lucky I was to have hours' worth of...you know if each of these memories was quick and I had hours of them. How fortunate was I?! And I didn't want to be sad, wanted to be grateful not sad. I'm still thinking about those memories and I will live with those memories in my heart and I will...love him forever".

Something that's become apparent to me whilst reading about both Chester Bennington and Chris Cornell's deaths are that social media has become a platform for sharing feelings. These aren't fans doing this, these are famous, successful musicians, feeling that they want and possibly need to put their emotions out there. Has this become a new way to tribute? A new release?

Chris Cornell struggled with addiction from around 1980 to roughly 1996 when his marriage broke up and his band Soundgarden disbanded. When talking about this period of his life, Chris Cornell said:

"I went through a serious crisis with depression where I didn't eat a whole meal every day. I was just kind of shutting down. I eventually found that the only way out of that was to change virtually everything in my life. That was a very frightening thing to do, but it was worthwhile."

To manage his addiction, he went into rehab in 2002 and reportedly managed to stay drug and alcohol free after that.

However, his wife who spoke to him the night before he was found dead said he sounded 'normal' and was making plans for their upcoming holiday. Chris was taking Benzodiazepines reportedly to control anxiety and depression but can have side effects leading to suicidal ideation.

During an interview in 1996, Chris talked very openly about feelings of depression and suicidal thoughts making it clear that he had a history of depression:

"I know what it feels like to be suicidal, and I know what it feels like to be hopeless.

There is some point where I learnt enough about myself to know that I don't have the tolerance to create other hurdles as well."

In an interview in 1999, he stated:

"No one really knows what run-of-the-mill depression is. You'll think somebody has run-of-the-mill depression, and then the next thing you know, they're hanging from a rope. It's hard to tell the difference. But I do feel that depression can be useful. Sometimes it's just chemical. It doesn't seem to come from anywhere. And whenever I've been in any kind of depression, I've over the years tried to not only imagine what it feels like to not be there but try to remind myself that I could just wake up the next day and it could be gone because that happens, and not to worry about it. And at the same time, when I'm feeling great, I remember the depression and think about the differences in what I'm feeling and why I would feel that way, and not be reactionary one way or the other. You just have to realize that these are patterns of life and you just go through them."

I spoke with Roisin, who worked in the music industry several years ago as mastering engineer and felt like she couldn't speak up about her mental health. Roisin had this to say. Thanks Roisin.

I worked in some great studios, mastering music that I believed in. I felt lucky. Then my Father died, and I just sank in to a massive depression. I couldn't do my work. I tried, but I couldn't do it. I desperately wanted to be 'normal' and feel as if I could manage everything. I had to admit in the end that I needed some time off. I told my manager at the company I worked for and I kid you not, he said 'when my mum died I was in work the next day. Take some time or whatever, but I can't guarantee there'll be work for you when you get back." I couldn't believe it, I was absolutely dumbstruck. I told people what he'd said, they told me to look for legal advice but my head wasn't ready. When I did go back to work after 6 weeks, he was really dismissive of me. He said there wasn't anything to work on and all the bigger projects had been given away. He said he'd call me. I was so depressed, I needed work as a distraction. I was really fortunate in that I had a few contacts in other companies and studios. I put the word out and ended up working for a lovely guy at a really great company down in Enfield. I just hadn't felt supported in my other job. I think that if my manager had been understanding, I probably would have felt better mentally and come back to work sooner too. Sadly, I think this is something that happens a lot in music. Managers and the powers that be know that people are desperate to work in music, so they have no problem letting someone feel like crap, you know? I do think there needs to be more awareness of mental health, in life generally and other industries.

I found it interesting that Roisin works in mastering, I'd never met a female masterer before (but that's another chapter!) and that she felt she wanted things to feel 'normal'. Roisin did start to recognise and accept that she needed some time and was let down when she needed support at the most difficult of times. Of course, more awareness for mental health issues is needed in all industries, but as we know that musicians are more prone to anxiety and depression, it's important to explore the possible reasons for this. Any manager in any organisation treating an employee like that is horrific. There certainly is a gap in resources for managers to gain knowledge on mental health and how to support employees.

Earlier in the chapter, we read a manager's comments that they aren't there to listen to the artist's problems and provide support, they're to exploit the artist. Perhaps musicians who have managers and record labels should be more aware of what they're getting themselves into? Maybe they need more knowledge on how things are run in the music industry and the callousness of which certain people operate? It could be that musicians who do suffer with mental health issues should keep away from the music industry if they can't handle it?

There are all comments that I've heard over the years from various people. 'You need to have a thicker skin' 'you're too nice' and all the rest. Perhaps they have a point, but if they do have a point, surely there must be some middle ground? I can try and be more think skinned mate, but do you think you could just be, well, nicer?

I asked the brilliant singer songwriter Hak Baker whether he thought that the music industry could be more supportive of musicians and their struggles;

"Course they could, but I feel we need to put the power back into our hands. Not being afraid of those feelings or emotions and embracing them. Being aware of them. What triggers them. And understand it. Work on it. People just need to feel comfortable to talk, but in this dog eat dog world it can be seen as weakness leaving yourself bare like that. There is a thin line unfortunately. No one trusts anyone."

This is a great point isn't it? People generally need to take more responsibility for their own mental health and be aware of their triggers. If you know you suffer from anxiety, you're aware that you might find touring difficult for instance, certain aspects of life away from home. It is the responsibility of the artist, musician and management to provide support and take responsibility for and help they may require.

Chester Bennington

Chester Bennington committed suicide In July 2017. He was the lead singer of the band Linkin Park. He was 41 when he died.

Since Chester Bennington's death, I've read a lot about him as a person, his mental health struggles and his close friendship with singer Chris Cornell who took his own life 2 months earlier. Chester was godfather to Chris Cornell's Son. When Chris Cornell died, Chester wrote on Instagram 'I can't imagine a world without you in it'. He also wrote an open letter to his friend after his death which is a heart breaking read.

> Dear Chris,
>
> I dreamt about the Beatles last night. I woke up with Rocky Raccoon playing in my head and a concerned look on my wife's face. She told me my friend has just passed away. Thoughts of you flooded my mind and I wept. I'm still weeping, with sadness, as well as gratitude for having shared some very special moments with you and your beautiful family. You have inspired me in many ways you could never have known. Your talent was pure and unrivalled. Your voice was joy and pain, anger and forgiveness, love and heartache all wrapped up into one. I suppose that's what we all are. You helped me understand that. I just watched a video of you singing 'A day in the life' by the Beatles and thought of my dream. I'd like to think you were saying goodbye in your own way. I can't imagine a world without you in it. I pray you find peace in the next life. I send my love to your wife and children, friends and family. Thank you for allowing me to be a part of your life.
>
> With all of my love.

By all accounts, Chester Bennington suffered from mental health issues before Chris Cornell's death and had been struggling with anxiety and depression for years. He had experienced addiction and during an interview before he died had stated:

"I know that for me, when I'm inside myself, when I'm in my own head... this place right here is a bad neighbourhood.

I should not be in there [my mind] alone. It's insane, it's crazy in here. It's a bad place to be by myself."

The rates for male suicide are statistically higher than women, and when a 'celebrity' ends their life, the fear is that it can influence others to do the same. However, when Kurt Cobain committed suicide in 1994, the rate of suicides dropped suggesting that there's an element of raising awareness, bringing suicide into the national consciousness and allowing people to talk about their feelings.

After her husband's death, Talinda Bennington set up a charity to raise awareness of mental health called' 320 Changes Direction'. This is her opening statement on the site-

"For 13 years I watched my husband Chester struggle with depression and substance use. I often felt scared and alone. I was uneducated about the challenges he faced, and I wanted information – but finding answers to my questions and available help for our family was very difficult.

We don't need to create more programs – there are good ones out there. But we do need to do two things. We need to streamline access to the help that IS available. And we need to change the culture of mental health so that those in need – and their family members – are able to speak openly about their struggles so that they can seek the care they deserve."

Powerful stuff, and so true. We need to raise awareness, we need to allow others to talk. Death, and suicide and addiction are such taboos- why? What are we afraid of?

If there is any positive aspect that has come out of this, it's the conversation that has arisen and the enabling of people feeling that they can talk about their mental health struggles and get the support they need.

I chose Chester Bennington and Chris Cornell to feature as Vignettes in this chapter, not because I feel that the industry was responsible for their suicides, but simply to highlight the lack of awareness of issues and also resources to help people struggling with depression. I think Chester Bennington's wife had an excellent point when she said that it's not about new resources, there are some brilliant ones out there already, it's about streamlining access to those services and also creating an environment where people feel able to talk about their mental health struggles.

This is what the book and this chapter is about, to shine a light on some issues, talk to people in the industry who've experienced depression, anxiety, stress, discrimination, addiction, and help raise awareness.

At one of the conferences I was asked to speak at, a man came over to me afterwards and said that he had been a signed artist and had now set up a record label of his own. He said he'd experienced the side of the industry that didn't support, and he wanted to turn that around.

Toby Marks has written a beautiful contribution. I was also fortunate enough to receive this from him especially for this chapter. These issues are something Toby feels strongly about and providing support for musicians who are suffering is something he feels passionately about. This is both harrowing and incredibly powerful, I'm humbled that he felt he wanted to share this:

When I first recovered the memory of being raped as a child I was at the peak of my career. My first two albums had topped the charts and the record company were eager for more. I had ridden the wave of success for a while, loving the feeling that things were getting better and better and always would. Yes, my ego loved the attention and adventure. And there was the endless stream of drugs and booze.

But... After a while I found the workload and constant demands too much and started to withdraw. It took me two years write that third album and partway through I recovered the rape memory. This experience changed the direction of my writing and it became the focus of the album. Once it was nearly ready the record label wanted to know how to sell it. What was it about? What did the title mean? Where was the hit single?

I was very raw at the time and had confided in just one person at the label. No one else noticed that I was going through anything though and our relationship became increasingly strained as I felt used and unsupported and they grew increasingly frustrated with the lack of easy marketing material.

I don't blame them individually for lacking sensitivity or failing to take care of me, they were just doing their jobs. But the culture of 90's independent record labels wasn't generally one, which nurtured the artists or even considered their emotional needs much, at least not in my experience.

I would hope that since then the industry has learnt that it's 'human assets' need to be looked after, that creativity often comes as part of a package of emotional fragility and vulnerability, and artists will at times need care and support. They may even need to be allowed to be 'unproductive' so that they can deal with their deeper needs, not just cater to the demands of the shareholders. Believe me, it will pay off in the long run.

A last thought for this section of the book: We need education on these issues available to everyone. There must be more information incorporated with music courses for students entering into the music industry. I see Music Business degrees and courses, but where is the mental health and wellbeing module? Everyone involved in the industry should be given the information on how to support and look after themselves and those around them. So, again, let's share the experiences we have. Let's show one another that we care, we can help and that there are resources out there to provide support.

•

Contributions

FLEXIE
MUSICIAN

Things have been tough for me and my family recently which has thrown a huge spanner in my music and creativity. Getting married was amazing but time and trying to build a family life had put a hold on things. Then when our boys were born and as they grew a little and became very musical (especially little Miika who had/ has an incredible singing voice for a toddler and Lonnee with his love for rhythm and grooves (he likes to breakdance a bit) I thanked the Lord I was able to give them something apart from life that they would be able to perhaps build upon and share with the world in a better and more successful way than their father. Then we discovered Miika's heart condition and that changed everything for a longtime in our lives as a family. Needless to say he has had his heart transplant but suffered a bleed and a stroke which made him lose his ability to talk (let alone sing or voice melodic tunes) and walk and is now undergoing rehab for brain injuries. As I write this I am sitting with him as he sleep at the brain rehab centre just about to do his 10pm medications for his heart. It has affected my family and friends in ways I cannot put into words. But the support from people throughout these last 9 months to a year has been immense and my family cannot express our gratitude enough.

I have been back home to Nigeria to perform for some huge events as headline artist and support, working with the industries finest and as crazy as it is, collected better pay for doing 3 songs over there than I have and would have working in the UK for 1 year. CRAZY HUH? And yet if I was to have had the opportunity to stay there for 6 months doing a video and just being on a tour as such, I would have killed it. Likewise if I had gone to the States (a few chances to have done so) I think with my personality and style of music I equally would have done well but who is to say?

I'm just going on feedback from various sources who heard my stuff a while ago and showed interest. Music is a funny one. My wife and I and I'm sure you do too as do a lot of our musical friends know of people who aren't very talented but have amassed huge success....why? Because the industry is full of BS. Funny thing is these individuals know they were very lucky and aren't good at all but again that's the world all over. Subsequently this and other factors have slowed my writing to a crawl. And producers who at first would jump on the opportunity to work with me due to my talent and skill are also under pressure to pay bills, mortgages etc and therefore now want money for everything when money was never an issue to begin with. I have numerous songs recorded and yet to be finalised simple because money is now an issue. So i have songs that my sons love and boogie or sing along to (in their own very cute way) at home or in the car (strangers too) that are not finished. Which is now making me feel like a failure as I don't want my boys to echo others by saying (You have some cool shit daddy what happened? Why aren't you out there doing what you love and do well?) I have friends who have also moved away from the UK to enhance their careers in music and that seemed to have worked for most of them but being in the UK doing a certain thing as a man of colour in a certain genre doesn't work. It's the old adage. I continue to do music as and when I can because of my undying love for the realism in music. But being real just ain't real enough. You gotta somehow be fake to bake the cake if you catch my drift.

—

FRAN WYBURN
SINGER, SONGWRITER

At 27 I sat on a beach whilst traveling around New Zealand and decided to be a songwriter. I knew it wouldn't be easy, but I felt it was something that gave me so much joy that I wanted to see what could happen if I pursued my love for it. In some ways I was attracted to it to test my own personal strength and will power, and I knew that it would potentially be something where I'd have to reach deep inside myself to continue with it. However, I don't think I'd ever fully anticipated just how much of a rollercoaster it would be and have discovered through doing it the importance of looking after my own wellbeing as my absolute priority above everything else and maybe this is the biggest gem that I have discovered. I was crippled with self-doubt and comparison for years and was forced to discover ways time and time again that would bring me back to my purpose. Things like being bold about wearing your heart on your sleeve, putting yourself out there in front of people who ultimately then have an opinion of what you're doing, having the confidence to trust yourself to finish ideas and be powerful about your choices and navigating working relationships with other musicians, producers, promoters etc has been one enormous journey into self-discovery where I feel I've been continuously pushed to my extremes. However I have survived and in actual fact even though at times my mental health has really been stretched I've found incredible coping methods like talking openly about my vulnerability, sharing that in my music, taking time to do a lot of self-love, learning little by little to have more and more faith in who I am. Recently I've had a massive break through with my relationship to my musician self-whilst I've been on the process of releasing my debut album. I believe there is only one thing that is real and truthful in all of this and that is the music- the emotional quality and communication of the ordered sound that you've chosen to order in that exact way, that's what's important and is always there to come back to, everything else from promoting yourself, to signing contracts, to making a strategy, to press etc is all the game of it. I will try to always come back to the heart in the music when I feel the rest of the game is getting me down. For me I feel music is where we discover ourselves and if that commitment to that expression of that is always there you have every right to take up that musical space and do your thing!!!!

—

HAK BAKER
SINGER, SONGWRITER

In 2016, Helpmusicians did a survey of over 2000 musicians, 76% said they'd suffered from anxiety and depression. Does this surprise you?

Nope not at all.

Have you ever suffered from depression and/or anxiety? Do you feel that being involved in the music industry has either helped or hindered your mental health?

If so, in what ways?

In both ways, it's a release for me as I ain't good at talking to people. Scared of feeling vulnerable you know. But, leaving yaself bare like that by writing so honest. Start getting a bit paranoid. Or you start realising certain feeling are there that you never knew was cause you're just tapping deeper and deeper into yourself. Feel like I owe the people that now. if that make sense

Do you feel that the music industry could be more supportive of musicians and their mental health struggles? In what ways could they provide support?

Course they could, but I feel we need to put the power back into our hands. Not being Afraid of those feelings or/and emotions and embracing them. Being aware of them. What triggers them. And understand it. Work on it. On your own as well as with potential help. People just need to feel comfortable to talk, but in this dog eat dog world it can be seen as weakness leaving yaself bare like that. There a thin line unfortunately. No one trusts anyone.

Does having a creative outlet help you when you're feeling low? Do you feel more creative at times where you may be suffering?

Yes and yes

When you've written and recorded a song, have you ever worried about what others are going to think of it? Does the validation of others matter when it comes to your music?

I have, but the people that feel it, They get it. That's it I don't care really.

Do you ever have to deal with 'bad' reviews or trolls regarding your music, if so, how does it effect you?

I don't pay it any mind.

Have you ever suffered from performance anxiety on stage and how do you deal with it?

Yeahhhh all the time. I get shaky and shit, then I drink it don't help quick enough but it does eventually. Get confident through. But nowadays I'm less anxious finally.

Now that you've reached a certain level of success, do you feel pressure to keep going? What would it mean to you if you were no longer signed to a label? Would you carry on writing and performing?

Yeah, pressure on myself. Cause I've decided I'm gonna do this so gotta prove myself right. I'm not signed im completely independent. I've never needed no cash lol to make money.

With certain songs such as 'Tom', they obviously affect you singing them on stage night after night and re living certain memories. How does singing emotionally significant songs affect you?

I ain't scared to be me so I'm ready to show them kind of feelings on stage. If I cry I cry it's cool. No biggy.

I went to see you perform in Manchester recently, stunning gig. You mentioned very openly on stage that you drink and smoke weed, do substances help you feel more creative? Or do you feel they block creativity?

They defo help they don't block at all. If I'm hanging I've more access to my feelings so I'm ready to write.

One of the chapters in the book is around race and mental health in the music industry. Do you feel that there are certain expectations put on you and your music as a black man in the music industry? How do you deal with the expectations put on you?

Yeahhh but i don't care about expectations. I do what I want. I don't care about what I'm supposed to do cause I'm black that's a joke. Stipulations are a joke and a trap and I ain't in it.

—

HEIDI DEWHURST
SINGER, SONGWRITER

I really wanted to be involved in this project, but at first, I didn't exactly know at what angle to come at my article from. Plenty of my friends have experienced issues with their mental health, and so have I. I know that this sort of thing seems to be prevalent amongst artists and I have my own theories on that, but that's all pretty much been covered.

As I sit here at my desk in my 9-5 (more like 9:35- 4:45 most days if I can get away with it) office job, I feel washed out and weary. It's 16:15 on a Monday afternoon and although I have got a decent amount of work done today, I feel distinctly unfulfilled. Usually Mondays go well, speeding by in a hazy mist of fresh determination and caffeine, but not today. I'm tired from the weekend- the beloved and seemingly illusive weekend. I have so many things to do as well as my office work- I need to compile that list of new releases for my friend Michael, I need to update the website for our songwriters' group, and I need to write that article for Rachel... and then I realise there is Youtube.

My fingers speed through the automatic movements to spell out my current obsession: Years and Years- 'Worship' (yes, I am late to every party as far as pop culture is concerned, but when I get on it, I am ON it.) My earphones flood my brain with music and subsequently serotonin, and all at once I feel revitalised. Perhaps the coffee has helped a bit, but this proves I definitely need music in my life- not only for emotional reasons and as an outlet, but to help me get things done.

* 'Lush life' follows in my playlist of recommended videos. I LOVE a bit of chart pop when I'm working. *

When I was a teenager I wrote an emo book. (Yes.) I wrote almost the whole thing listening to Muse. (I later found out that Stephanie whatshername had done exactly the same with Twilight- I swear I was not influenced by her...) I found that whilst music was coursing through my mind, I could come up with new ideas inspired by, but not stolen from the songs I was listening to. This is because of the feelings they gave me, not the content per se. By the same token I find that I can write lyrics or poetry best when I am listening to music. Odd? Perhaps. It sounds as though it wouldn't work- you'd get distracted- but it does.

I think music and the arts are drastically overlooked in today's society, and especially in education. My own experiences cement in me a belief that taking part in creative activities is an essential part of a person's development. When all is said and done, the power that a song has to relax, inspire and awaken should not be overlooked, nor should it be taken for granted. So much good can come from music whether listening to, writing or performing it.

—

KARL WALSH
SINGER, SONGWRITER, PRODUCER

With regard to whether the creative process helps at all when one is feeling low, when the black dog is curled around our feet. I would say that sometimes, writing out of melancholy I have provided something of a cure but whether this might work for a deeper depression I have my doubts.

Essentially the biggest problem I have with the black dog is that it stops me from doing anything positive. It is famous for robbing us of energy and the desire to act on anything. The type of melancholy that inspires wistful poetry and love songs is not really the kind of heavy depression that some of us find so debilitating.

As far as alcohol is concerned I'm with Shakespeare when he puts these words into the mouth of the drunken porter in Macbeth *"It provokes the desire, but it takes away the performance. Therefore, much drink may be said to be an equivocator with lechery. It makes him, and it mars him; it sets him on, and it takes him off; it persuades him, and disheartens him; makes him stand to and not stand to; in conclusion, equivocates him in a sleep, and, giving him the lie, leaves him."*

I have written many a chart-blasting song under the influence of a bottle of red and then lost the paper I wrote it on! Without doubt some of the best poetry arrives with the dregs at the bottom of the bottle but all of the work required to turn that poetry into a communicable piece of art are almost impossible without a clear head.

For many years I bought the line about the crazy artists half drunk on absinthe producing art that only dangerous and brave boys could produce throwing their health out of the window for a glimpse of the muse. Our heroes were all dead. Jim Morrison, Jimi Hendrix, Janice Joplin, Amy Winehouse, Ian Curtis. Live fast die young was the plan but people seldom point out that most of these young people only turned to drink to avoid the pressure of success. It wasn't the drink that brought them success.

I try so hard when working to avoid cliché, to avoid the obvious and yet quite a lot of what makes popular song is familiarity, the sense that it sounds like something we already like or reminds us of a classic in some way. So, it is hard not to hope that someone will feel this way about that new song. I have honestly been so moved when performing a song for the first time (generally to a friend or band fellow) that I have almost broken down before the end. The emotional catharsis is that great it can almost be too much. Of course, it matters what people think of what we do! If you have chosen a life where your entire self-worth is measured by how good that song is then the response you get for it everything.

We once had the most hilarious review in the NME for a single we brought out on Factory Records way, long ago, and back further still, The reviewer didn't like it at all but really enjoyed an extended metaphor. He cast my band as a newly exhumed 'hippy zombie' that needed to be put back in its grave and the soil firmly beaten down over our heads! It was such an evil review that made me shrink inside. I wanted to find the guy and kill him! As time passed I started to laugh and as you can see I have now entirely forgotten about it.

Regarding image, I think this feeds into the basic human desire to be liked but as with everything else, when you become an artist of any sort the process is coloured by the stage. Even the most exaggerated scruff does not appear that way by accident. (even if they believe they do) There was a lot of talk about Bowie and his constant re-invention but I think that this was a function of him growing and changing as a person. If we look at any artist with longevity it is possible to track their development and cherry pick certain looks that typified certain albums or songs. At the very least (something that Bowie would definitely agree with) it is good marketing.

As time passes the kind of look that suits a bewildered teen with nothing to do but cry about how unfair the world is (See 'the charts' from 79' to 99') does not look quite as cool on a grown up (same people charts 89' to present day.) As my dear friend Matt Jones, the Pixies sound engineer often says; *"You've got to be buff to be a scruff."*

When I first began singing in a band I wanted to change the world. Before Geldof and before Bono all I wanted was to be a kind of Jesus (possibly in black leather trousers). No-one was listening to politicians but they would listen to my songs and the world would agree to end all war and feed the starving children.

Today I feel pretty good if a handful of people like our music. Some years ago, a young couple told me that they had one of my songs as their morning alarm. *"It's music that gets us through the day."*

I consider it worthwhile now if I can entertain for 3 minutes. A tiny drop in the ocean, a speck of dust but at least something. Peter Cook and Dudley Moor made a brilliant film called Bedazzled. In it young Dud gets tempted by the diabolical Cook into increasingly absurd situations in return for his soul. Every time Dud thinks that he's getting what he wanted the Devil's exasperating trick is revealed. The Devil promises Dudley a life of bliss surrounded by women, cut to Dudley in the Convent!

We have the internet, we have our own record company, we have the tech to make an album in our bedroom and release it to the world. So does everybody else! We can write the song, sing the song, and produce the song and keep all ninety nine percent (never one hundred) of the income from the song. Hoorah! What will you do with that .2 pence? Just like Dud we have been given exactly what we asked for never realising that it was not what we needed. All of the freedom in the world (musically speaking) is of no use whatsoever to your career if nobody knows who you are. The mechanics of Origination are now entirely in the hands of the artist but dissemination relies on marketing and marketing costs money. This makes the question a much bigger one about who has all the money!

No matter how nervous you feel before a show the moment the first chords are struck the nerves melt away. There just isn't space in the consciousness to harbour freeloaders like nerves when there is work to be done! It is true that nerves can become a problem if you are only playing infrequently. Each gig feels like the Albert Hall and it is hard to relax. That said everybody knows that nerves are only a sign that you are taking the job seriously. Alcohol might give you the impression that you are relaxed but generally booze just makes players sloppy. (It also plays havoc with the nerves of everybody else in the band!)

Stage fright, nerves and blind panic? No never had them. One evening I was walking across Leicester Square with the band and our manager. He had done the impossible job of arranging a show case for Sony and EMI and Virgin and Island and Mother and… you get the picture. (There used to be big record companies that could change your life!) I had new boots on. I had new gear. I was artfully scruffy. We had been for a drink to settle the nerves but as we walked across that square I prayed to God. *"Please God! Let there be an earthquake... let the tower of London fall! Let me be swallowed whole. Anything! Please God! Just this once don't make me have to do this..."*

As I walked my knees were weak and my smile was thin. An hour later I was on that stage dry mouthed and sick with fear, my guitar strapped on and a set of new songs at my feet.

We started to play.

—

KEL PAGE
SINGER OF THE EMPTY PAGE

I think it's quite a hard thing to pick apart. Does our mental health suffer because we are musicians or are we musicians because our suffering from mental health problems makes us more creative? Most (but not all) people I know who are musicians have some kind of mental health problems or have had at some point in their lives. I think that, rather than musicianship being a cause of mental health issues, it's more something that people do to help them to cope.

Personally, I have struggled with anxiety and depression for about 20 years and music has been a lifeline for me. I find that writing songs, especially writing lyrics, helps me to get my feelings down on paper. Often, they are temporary feelings, and it feels weird to look back on them in black and white. I think it helps to know that you don't always feel like that, to look at it from a distance helps you to see it more clearly. Many of the songs I have written over the past 20 years have been about struggles with mental health. I think it's been an extremely useful tool for me to cope better. However, the industry itself contains a lot of factors which I think have had a negative impact on my mental health and that of others.

Being constantly held up for criticism has been extremely difficult for me. When you pour your heart and soul into something and then a bad review tears it apart, that can be very hard to take. I still find that difficult to cope with. I've had to learn to use constructive criticism to make me a better writer, but it's hard to know what to do with the stuff that's not constructive, just cruel. Over the time I have been in a band the internet has become all powerful, and that means that now everyone's a critic, which is something else which most definitely has a negative effect on creators. I've always been able to participate in the party side, the drugs and alcohol etc. without having any problems with addiction or anything like that, I can take it or leave it and generally don't go crazy, but I know many, many other musicians for whom the drugs and alcohol have had a catastrophic effect. I know non-musicians in this situation too though.

I think the constant criticism definitely causes problems, I have seen this in struggling and in relatively successful musicians. Also, it's extremely difficult, if not impossible, to make a living from writing and performing original music. I know hundreds of musicians with varying levels of success and most of them have a day job, many of them have a crap day job too because it's hard to commit to a 'proper' job and be able to take time off for touring etc. For me that's been really hard. I've always been skint, I've always until very recently had minimum wage, casual jobs. Virtually every holiday I have taken from work over the past 15 years or so has been to go on tour, which doesn't seem like a bad thing to an outsider but it means you never get an actual break. I took a year off music recently to go travelling because I realised that I had had virtually no holidays in over a decade, so I saved up for a few years from my minimum wage job, money that in the past would have been spent on making an album or something and spent it on travelling instead. I had a lot of guilt about it, but I'm glad I did it because I was starting to resent the fact that every spare moment and every spare penny I had went on the cottage industry of my band, which never made a profit and was just constantly in a cycle of debt and repayment. We have spent thousands of our own money on making records, rehearsing, touring etc., sometimes barely breaking even and sometimes just having to write it off, even though we have sold thousands of records too! So yeah, financial worries are a big cause of stress and anxiety. A lot of people also get very depressed about a feeling of failure because they have never had the kind of success people had in the 80s. I used to have that problem too and it does creep back in sometimes, but I have done a lot of thinking, soul searching and looking at the facts of what has happened in the industry in the past 20 years with the internet, and evaluating my own achievements and I don't feel like a failure at all most of the time.

When I was younger I think I associated success with making a living and measured it by record sales and gig attendance. All those things are hard to get past, but record sales have changed dramatically in the industry since I started writing songs in the 90s. The way people consume music has changed, and also the amount of people making music has grown exponentially. In the past, people had to go to gigs to buy the music, they had to buy the music on hard copy to hear it even, I remember the uproar that there was about people making taped copies of albums, that it was killing music. Now it's beyond anything we could have ever imagined then. The younger generations see music as something that's just there, accessible everywhere all the time at the push of a button. I think my generation and those above me have had an extremely hard time making sense of the changes in the way people consume music, because it was such a labour of love for fans in the past, you had to really make an effort to get involved in being a fan, it's so easy now and that seems to devalue music almost, not just in a financial sense.

I think these changes in the industry have definitely affected the mental health of myself and my peers, because the goalposts have constantly been moved. But you must move with the times, this is where we are and there is no changing it. I had a eureka moment about this a few years ago where I forced myself to completely let go of my old ideas about success. My ethos for almost 10 years has been that music and making money are completely separate issues in my life. I have worked on getting better jobs so that I can be happier and more relaxed about my personal finances and day to day existence. I do this so that I can keep music as something pure, something I do for its creative value to myself and anyone who's listening, rather than something I do to try and make a living while I struggle to make ends meet. This has freed me mentally in a big way. Of course, having to have a day job 40 hours a week leaves less time for music making, and it would be lovely not to have to do that, but I think I am a better, more interesting writer because the jobs I have done at least, have value in themselves as sources of creative ideas, and I spend a bit less time worrying about money which means I can think about other things. I'm not that much better off, I hasten to add, but I do think my day to day life is more pleasant these days and that helps me to relax and be creative in different ways. The main thing now that gets me down is that I just would like more people to hear my music, I'd like to reach more people with it because anyone who makes music or art, I believe, makes it as a communicative thing, so the more people you can communicate with through your music, the better. I admit, having more people listening to my music would be good for my ego too. So that's the battle now, to get heard by more people, and sometimes that still brings me down because it's really hard in such a saturated world. I'm currently working on my ego and trying to stop it from ruling me as much as it does though, I think that's where a lot of my current mental health issues come from.

I think 'tortured souls', deeper thinkers, are more creative, and that the meditation involved in being creative make you ruminate a lot, which inevitably leads to being more of a tortured soul! One hand washes the other! As far back as I can remember I have been someone who overthinks, worries and asks a lot of big questions. I recall writing songs of my own from as young as about 6 years old, so I really can't say which one, if any, came first. I'd venture that they are inextricably linked. I do know for certain, as I took some time off music in the first few months of travelling, for the first time ever, that I can't live without making music. Listening to it helps a lot, but it's not enough, I have to create it. I'm certain that my mental health problems would have consumed me completely by now if I didn't have that creative outlet and the opportunity to let out that primal scream as a singer on a regular basis too.

—

LEVI CUSS
SINGER- SONGWRITER

I woke up in an apartment in the middle of Berlin, probably one of the trendier, sections of town, really living my dream. But truly wondering what I was doing and doubting I could carry on the pace at which, it took to get me here. I am a Canadian musician who has painfully been making the transition from a Carpenter to a fulltime musician. At this point I had been on the road for the last two years and the last three months working my way through mainland Europe with little budget and zero support. I had released a record in the UK that was doing surprisingly well, charting briefly on the UK blues charts, getting a ton of radio play and getting some really great reviews in some great UK music magazines……Living the dream…… Right? My friends and family back home were so proud of me, and on the outside, I looked bullet proof. The problem being, I was still miserable, I needed more, I needed help, I wanted support, but there was none. Living my dream was one of the darkest loneliest times of my life, it seems impossible to say that. But the same great voice in my head that write's these great songs is the same great voice there rips me to shreds and fights my focused from moving forward and getting better. Maybe I have a new dream now, maybe it's still the same. The harder and further I chase the dream, the further away it seems to be. Staying true to yourself and pushing yourself to be authentic will take its toll on you, but it's probably good for your music. I wish I had some easy answers to catching your dreams and being happy about them, but I don't. I think being honest and talking about it and keep putting one foot in front of the other, is your best bet.

Thanks- Levi Cuss

—

LISA MARIE GLOVER
SINGER- SONGWRITER

I am guilty.

I am guilty because I am lucky to have a creative outlet when many people do not.

Yet despite this, I get envious when I listen to BBC Radio 6 because it would appear that there are plenty of independent and interesting musicians who are more successful than I am. When I'm in the 'dark place' the slightest mention of a more successful songwriter who may be touring and playing at whichever prestigious venue can plunge me into depression and I am ready to give it all up. The slightest rejection can also make me want to hide under a duvet. Forever.

I am guilty because I am whinging over a lack of success compared to what I would like to have despite having a roof over my head and not having to worry where my next meal is coming from. What the hell makes me so special that I should get to do my dream job when so many other embittered people I've worked in offices with do not?

I am guilty of battling with low self-esteem. It's hard to keep a sense of self-worth when you find yourself at a gig where you have to stop playing to hold a speaker steady while a fight breaks out. Maybe you are told to shut up in a hotel bar mid song while the TV is turned up so that the rude people in question can watch sport, regardless of the people who are listening. Both of these things have happened to me whilst performing.

I'm not saying that it's bad all of the time; sometimes it's great and I have made a lot of good friends through music. This is just how I feel when I am on a bad day. I am embarrassed by those feelings and I think they are linked to a green eyed seven-year-old girl inside of me who also probably throws board games up in the air when she is losing.

I keep doing music for some reason. I don't really think I have a choice in the matter. I am obsessed and it's creepy.

—

LOUIS BARABBAS
SINGER-SONGWRITER AND FOUNDER OF DEBT RECORDS

You've probably heard that success can go to your head. Perhaps it's there already. But what about failure, where does that go? Maybe into our bones, weighing them down as we trudge towards a receding goal? Or our stomachs, churned into acidic geysers of resentment? Or is failure more interested in the heart, spreading like ivy on a monument, patiently worming its roots into each imperceptible crack until one thoughtless tug turns the whole thing to rubble?

Our ever-present notion of ever-absent success has a lot to answer for. It is both the carrot and the stick, the treasure and the map. Of all the forces that can unsettle a creative mind, the pursuit of success (or the dread of failure) is a particularly caustic one – a woolly abstract phenomenon found across all disciplines, though manifested in myriad forms and flavours – at best it is distracting, at worst devastating.

Yet we can't seem to reach a consensus on what success in the creative sector actually is. There are plenty of gauges to measure it by: money, fame, awards, happiness, sustainability, a body of work, a full diary, the respect of one's peers, the recognition of strangers... but individually none of these factors are exclusive to the successful, nor are they necessarily forbidden the unsuccessful. Indeed, this ambiguity can sometimes be a comfort. What songwriter hasn't at some point in their career fortified their morale with the idea that a lack of popularity is a sign of integrity? Unfortunately it isn't just ourselves we must convince of this, but everyone else as well. We might meet someone who applies a different set of scales to the scrutiny of our achievements, who doesn't realise how successful we are on our own terms and inadvertently causes our fragile nexus of beliefs to disintegrate with a single Mozart comparison. Maybe that is real success: the power to include others in our private spectrums, so they regard us the way we're supposed to be seen, however fantastically.

But the big problem isn't how we measure this slippery construct, or even how we define it. But rather to what degree we let it loom in the Venn diagram of our work and life. What exactly is on trial here? Our art? Our choices? Our standing in the industry? Our place in society? Ourselves?

Those who are moved to crisis or despair by such abstract pressures tend to be reacting to an external concept of success rather than a personal one. Because success is everywhere. Never in the history of human endeavour has it been so present. There's seemingly a new "Tips For Success in Music" article every day and a new set of industry expectations every month. We are all endlessly self-editing our public activities in Realtime, buffing up gemstones sifted from the common slurry of each day. We know we do it, but we forget everyone else does it too. So everywhere we turn, there it is: other people's success, deafening us, absorbed by a presumed multitude while our poor facsimiles of achievements disappear into the void.

Almost all artists are defeated by success in one way or another – whether smothered by too much of it or starved by too little. But when examined closely success and failure turn out to be all symptoms and no sickness, a shared hallucination enabled by an industry that has always thrived on deception, fuelled by our eagerness to be deceived, invited by our own naively treacherous sensitivity and its constant cravings for encouragement/acceptance. Our private insecurities are forced to bloat and swell in isolation rather than allowed to mingle with their ugly little counterparts festering inside the minds of our equally vulnerable contemporaries.

We play the notes in the order we choose, we set the words to the music or the music to the words, we express ourselves and combine with others to make that expression influence and illuminate the world around us. At these things we rarely fail. And yet we voluntarily place ourselves in a game of ever-shifting rules where failure is the only certainty. It is not enough to stay true to one's own definition of success, because nothing in creativity is ever static, we will always find new ways to undermine our sense of self-worth, or allow outside influences to undermine it for us. The only way to conquer the spectre of success is by working together, sharing experiences, expressing doubts, helping others and accepting help in return. Art is all about communication and yet artists are all too often the worst communicators. Here are two famous clichés about success: "Success is a state of mind" and "It's lonely at the top". But if we discuss how we feel about failure, what we fear versus what we want, who we admire and what we envy, how we would like to be rather than how we want to be perceived, then that "state of mind" singular can become a "state of minds" plural, and before we know it, the top isn't all that lonely anymore. That'll be the day when we can finally stop wasting our talents on the trivial concerns of our fickle industry and get on with fathoming the deeper miseries of life, which is what artists are really good at.

—

MIRANDA ARIEH
SINGER-SONGWRITER, CAMPAIGNER

Music and Mental Health

SO, what came first- the music or the mental illness? It's a question which has long plagued professionals acknowledging the link between creativity and mental health. Are people who are experiencing mental health or emotional issues more drawn to creating art and music as a way of being able to express themselves when a simple sentence can't? Or are 'creative types' more likely to experience mental health struggles due to the lack of creativity in modern society's working lives and the tricky path to being able to make your art a sustainable career?

My story

My name's Miranda and I'm a singer songwriter from Leeds, UK. I first picked up a guitar (with only one string to speak of) when sectioned into in an adolescent psychiatric unit for 9 months at the age of 14, bridging the gap between me being placed in safe houses and foster care after running away from an abusive home. I had been over dosing repeatedly and self-harming prior to my admission. Singing/music and writing songs was a deep pleasure of mine from as early as I can remember, and I was always very creative from a young age. Although I wasn't officially taught any instruments growing up, we had a piano in the house which I used to play about on and I would write countless poems and lyrics every single day.

Throughout the 9 months I was in Highroyds Hospital I was given lots of therapy and medications of uppers and downers, (not forgetting the tranquilizers; used for when I became too excited from the uppers they had given me..) Many of the drugs they forced me to take in there have since been banned for under 18's. Out of all the 'treatments' that I was given, nothing quite seemed to work as well as me sitting down with the guitar. Playing, singing, and writing lyric after lyric after lyric. This, to me, was the only way I could properly express what I was feeling and describe what was going on for me. It felt like a release; a relief, a way to open up when I had felt so closed.

When I was discharged from hospital this carried on. I joined a punk band, Mutiny, at the age of 16 and then went on to play in several different Leeds based bands. I started out as a solo artist in 2016 and am due to release my debut solo album Ferine in 2018. I am so drawn to writing songs I would go as far as to say that I couldn't function without that privilege and feel I get a lot more poorly when I am not creating. For me, singing and songwriting don't feel like just a hobby or something that I just enjoy, it feels like a need, a must, a vital part of who I am.

Writing from feeling, not thinking

Being creative certainly helps me manage my mental health, however I don't feel that I write for myself anymore. I write to help others and create music to express and evoke emotion, whether that's a light hearted thoughtful reaction or an emotion of 'I get it, I understand, it's OK'. I have written many songs to empower others and many about mental health itself. Sometimes I like to create a character and write a story in my songs. Sometimes I write a song to someone in my life who I am having difficulties communicating to, and sometimes I just write for the sheer fun of playing with words and a melody. There are no two songs that are the same! But I write them all from feeling and not thinking. This is why I feel I may also be drawn to songwriting. I feel so mindful when I am doing it. I am so in the moment that I can get lost in it for hours. It quietens my often wildly busy mind. I can focus so clearly on writing and feeling and music alone and find this the most uniquely soul nourishing and healing thing.

The impact on mental health as a gigging musician.

Striving to create a sustainable music career comes at a price for many musicians. Gigging endlessly has its pros but there may be many late nights in loud bars and in the least sober of atmospheres. Many musicians may go into music feeling fab- but the late nights, nerves and low pay can take their toll. I often feel like I become very vulnerable when I get up on stage, that I am bearing my heart and soul and it is a risk! But that's part of why I do it! I wouldn't wish for any other career than to create, perform, sing, and play, despite the vulnerabilities, but I can understand how many musicians get burned out so fast due to even sheer practicalities. For example- having to go to work late at night on a regular basis.

It has been very important to me personally to define what exactly success looks like to me in a very realistic as possible way. (Without stifling my dreams!) This can prove a real challenge; however, I have come out with the same goal again and again: to simply be able to do more and more of what I love the most.

Afterthought.

What would it look like if everyone struggling with mental illness were given the opportunity and encouragement to paint how they are feeling or write some lyrics to express themselves or sing their heart out about their pain and confusion. Do we develop as a 'creative' if the pre-disposition for emotional struggles are there or are we simply ALL creative beings and some of us have the privilege of opportunity to be around instruments and such like? I feel we are all creative beings, just some of us feel the need and drawn to tap into that form of self-expression more than others. And some are simply never shown that opportunity on their path. There are plenty of musicians without mental health problems of course, but I suppose we will never know- is it actually their creativity and self-expression that have kept them well?!!

—

NICK J TOWNSEND
MUSICIAN

My name is Nick J Townsend. I am a musician and I was diagnosed with Clinical Depression somewhere between my mid 20's. It's hard to remember exactly all the events that led up to me first visiting a Doctor for him to label me with this condition and then for me to accept a treatment of prescription drugs but I obviously wasn't happy. My life changed the moment a Doctor diagnosed me. Around this time I lost my job, had my heart broken by a girlfriend and fell out with a band member who had slept with that same girlfriend behind my back. My music career seemed up in the air at that point too because of it. Well after drinking, drugs and other distractions I ended up in a sorry state and didn't feel like carrying on with life; next thing I know my wonderful kind landlady at the time getting me into a taxi to take me to the hospital to commit myself for rehabilitation so that I was under watchful eyes. I was in there for a few weeks. I managed to convince them it was safe for me to go home but when I returned the world seemed noisier than before. I was now on medication, diagnosed as clinically depressed, out of work and on income support. I tried to get back to my old self, started being creative again and my Doctor bless him even told me that music makes me happy so I should do it. I started to get my confidence back, even started dating again but there was always this feeling of anxiety all the time and I couldn't work out what I could do to ever stop it. I ended up meeting a lovely lady and I found myself feeling comfortable with starting a full time relationship with her; I was smiling again, my music career was getting back on track, my social life was back and things seemed to be going well. Every day was still as hard to cope with and I just had difficulty in not feeling depressed. However, it actually took my life going further downhill to really combat depression. In time my relationship with this woman finished, she hadn't the same feelings for me anymore; I was completely devastated but it was amicable to an extent. Amazingly my benefits stopped the week after, my partner said I was welcome to stay whilst I get back on my feet but it became impossible to live in the same home with her anymore so I had to go and I then became faced with the prospect of being homeless and had now no income. Now what happened next was strange; everything seemed to be going wrong again and in the back of my mind I thought "Oh my depression is so going to flare out of control" but the truth is I didn't actually have any time to even think about depression. My life was about to reset all over again and it was important to stay focused and deal with my situation. I left town, found a job within two days, had to sofa surf for a bit but I had no time to wallow as every day ahead of me was a such a climb and a mission; arranging my journey to work, where I was staying the night, what food I could afford and how to survive. It was at this time something crucial occurred to me - my childhood. I was completely unhappy as a child; there wasn't a word like depression when I was young and it made sense that perhaps I'd always been depressed. It was the Doctor that first diagnosed me as clinically depressed which helped me believe that I'd developed a condition and in my mind that had been where it all began to go tits up. The reality is that I've always been depressed, I just never had a name for it when I was growing up. That actually made me feel a huge sense of relief. For some reason, me realising that I've always been depressed made me extremely happy. That was ten years ago. I've not looked back. Some days are better than others for sure but I feel great. My music career has really blossomed since this way of looking at depression. I can't explain it and I don't see a need to because I'm happy with who I am. I guarantee that there are bad days and good days ahead of me but I will always be that same unhappy child who managed to find sparks of hope in order to move forward despite whatever life threw at him next. I'm not clinically depressed. I was born depressed. That makes me happy and I'm not in the dark any longer.

—

PETE WILSON
GUITARIST: STEVE IGNORANT'S SLICE OF LIFE

Being a musician was all I ever really wanted to do from the time when you realistically think about how you want your life to turn out. I can honestly say that I have achieved more than I ever thought I could but not as much as I hoped I would. I feel very lucky to have got to where I currently am and I know that if it all went away tomorrow I would be grateful for where I managed to get rather than being bitter about what I didn't manage to achieve.

I suffered with mental health issues and alcoholism long before I first joined a band and properly started down the path I'm currently on. I was a relatively late starter in bands in that I was around 25 before joining a band that got together weekly to rehearse and subsequently gigged around the country attempting to get somewhere as musicians. By the time I joined this band I was already an alcoholic and had suffered from depression since my late teens. The belief that I have is that art and music can attract people who have these issues rather than causing these issues in the first place.

The tough and sometimes heart-breaking nature of the music industry can certainly exacerbate these issues but that can I don't believe they cause them. Personally I never felt connected to what would be classed as mainstream society. I felt like an outsider (as many teenagers do) and wanted no part of the normal life that I saw all around me. I remember being shocked when, at 18, I realised that I was the only one of my friends who did not intend to go to university. It was just accepted by the rest of my friends however I wanted something different, something more.

I think it only fair to say at this point that I'm currently approaching 40 and have a full-time office job while also regularly performing in a professional band. I've been lucky enough to have toured around the UK, Europe, Australia and New Zealand and performed memorable gigs at places I love such as The Hop and Grape and The Ritz in Manchester along with The Electric Ballroom, The Forum and Shepherd's Bush Empire in London. The highlight of my career so far would have to be playing Glastonbury in 2017. I saw Bowie play there in 2000 and I thought about this for the whole of our set. It was an incredible and unforgettable moment. Throughout all of this though, I still had to maintain a full time job. This highlights the difference between what I would class as "making it" and not, to put it bluntly. Being a full time musician without the need of any supplementary income, whether that be a full or part time job was my ultimate goal. It was a very strange experience for me to have played a stunning gig to a sold out Shepherd's Bush Empire on a Saturday night back in 2011 only to be back in work as normal on the Monday morning. This juggling act can be very difficult sometimes.

This juxtaposition can be one of the factors that leads to exacerbating the mental health issues that come with this lifestyle. It can often feel like you're working 2 full time jobs which can be exhausting even when things are going well. It can be crushing when they are not. I spent about a year recently questioning whether I wanted to spend all my free time travelling around the country feeling unfulfilled and potentially wasting my time. I was very close on numerous occasions to just leaving it all behind. I thought that maybe this would help with all my other issues. If I wasn't pursuing some impossible goal then maybe I wouldn't feel the pain of not achieving it. Maybe it would help me finally grow up and accept the responsibility of being an adult, something which I and others believe many musicians avoid. Throughout this time however, I knew deep down that I couldn't leave it behind. I couldn't not play the guitar or listen to music or go to gigs. I wasn't ready to let it all go. Maybe there will come a time in the future when I want to do that but thankfully, right now I have no desire to.

I want to highlight that I am in an incredibly lucky situation. I have the full support of a wonderful partner who just wants the best for me, my job is flexible enough for me to get all the time off I require to perform regularly and the band I'm in is like a family that is currently loving the journey we're on. So long it works for everyone involved then we will continue for as long as we can. I am fortunate in that I do not worry about what people outside of my inner circle think about my lifestyle. For a long time all I really wanted was to be confident that I had tried my hardest to be proud of how I lived my life and pursued my goals. Yes, I could have tried harder to push myself as a guitarist, to learn more in terms of recording and mixing. There is always something that you could be doing to further yourself but, when opportunities came my way I have always thrown myself fulling into making sure I made the most of them and thankfully a lot of them have paid off. Making myself proud has always meant more to me than impressing other people.

It's impossible to say whether I would have been happier if I had not been a musician. I managed to stop drinking and have been sober for 4.5 years. Good going considering you're always around alcohol at gigs and on the road. I don't have the feeling of wasting my life at the moment. I'm happy with the amount of time that I spend away with the band while also having plenty of time for myself. I'm realistic enough to know that I'm never going to be in the situation where I can quit my job to do this full time but, even if that did happen I believe that I would still carry the demons that have been with me for that last 25 years. It may well be that being a musician has helped me in this respect. It gave me an outlet that other people sometimes struggle to find. Yes, sometimes it's amazingly frustrating but when it's good it can be magical.

—

POLLY PAULUSMA
SINGER- SONGWRITER

During the course of any professional life, it can be a challenge to maintain that thin veneer of professionalism when we are incapacitated by circumstances such as illness, family commitments, pregnancy, or bereavement. But in other more regulated industries, there seem to be better-honed support networks in place to catch people when they fall. In my experience of the music industry, that is not obviously the case. Having a baby was a terrifying gamble of economics for me; like many working would-be parents I faced the stark choice of 1) making more money than my partner, 2) making enough money to pay for some childcare, or 3) taking a pause my music-making career. So, as I expected baby number one, I threw myself into my work; I recorded my second album at enormous expense to my small record label and committed to three 2-week tours (two in the UK, one in Italy) by the time my baby was 9 months old. What I didn't expect was post-natal depression, which I experienced during the second tour, when my baby was about 6 months old. I'd heard so many friends and family members describing their own symptoms of clinical depression, but it was an eye-opener to experience it first-hand. One morning I woke up and it was as if I had been surrounded by a milky-white mist. All tasks had suddenly become Herculean, impossible to complete. I went to a supermarket to buy some basics, and emerged blinking three hours later with nothing. Lists became tangles of confusion-web. And I was meant to be touring. The only way through it was for my husband, who had taken time off work to care for our baby while I was on stage, to take over. He organised my set lists, assembled my instrument setups, plugged together my jack leads, got my plectrums and picks organised and then literally pushed me out onto the stage. I felt like a zombie, an emptiness out there before people. Sometimes I remembered my words, sometimes whole songs collapsed under me like a house of cards. I felt completely absent. I had to cancel some shows, but I soldiered on through too many of them, in a state of half-wakefulness. At the end of the tour, I went to talk to my GP; despite her assurances that it would not cross over, I was reluctant to take medication because I was still breastfeeding. She advised a couple of weeks of real, proper sleep first, and to take the pills if that didn't work. In the end the sleep proved very effective; I woke up one morning, about a month after it had begun, and the mist had miraculously lifted. Suddenly I could once again follow a sequence of instructions A-B-C-D-E in linear fashion through to a conclusion. It felt like a miracle. I am grateful for having had the experience of such a physical feeling; it has given me greater empathy with all the amazing people around me who have to deal with depression day in, day out. But I was very scared at the time because there is such (financial, emotional, personal) pressure on you — and you put so much pressure on yourself — as a musician to perform — the show must go on, whatever the cost. You don't get paid unless you heave yourself onto that stage and go through the motions, and there is little tolerance for 'lame' excuses. I had never cancelled a show before and I felt that as a woman and new mum I needed to prove my stamina and worth. But I don't know now what I was trying to prove, and to whom. Looking back, I would have been really grateful for some expert guidance for new parents in the music industry about how to look after yourself and baby, how to protect yourself from over-exhaustion and burnout, and perhaps more structured support in terms of maternity benefits and subsidised childcare for those in the creative industries.

—

SEBASTIAN
MUSICIAN, PSYCHOTHERAPIST

When I was 34, my band broke up. It was a mutual thing: no big controversy; we were just pulling inexorably in different directions. But it was heart-breaking nonetheless. I knew that it would have taken me forever to find another group of musicians of that calibre, so I decided to throw in the towel – or at least, give up my ambitions of "making it". While I'd certainly had more downs that ups in my life, I'd never experienced what you might call "a depression", but all of a sudden there it was: for several days I could barely get out of bed; meanwhile, I developed a food phobia that lasted considerably longer. Luckily for me, my wife was very understanding. Much more than me, had "always feared this day would come". But she could just as easily have ridiculed me, since throughout more than ten years' toil, my music had barely registered on anyone's radar.

Giving up my musical career was a traumatic upheaval for various personal reasons that aren't particularly generalizable. But some other observations may be instructive:

- I'm so thankful that the band broke up when I was 34, not 39. When you have a 'do or die' attitude like I did, the stakes get higher as the years pass. Nowadays I think you can be just as committed – indeed, committed more effectively – to a goal without being so nihilistic.

- Keeping a band together, especially in the face of anonymity, is REALLY stressful. With us, for example, the problem was always holding onto a drummer. Trying to keep everyone motivated, coming to rehearsal, etc., while coping with personnel instability and navigating the creative process (which inevitably creates friction) wore me out much more than I realised at the time.

- Likewise, organising and playing gigs independently is exhausting. The big surprise for me, after the band broke up, was that I didn't miss performing at all – what I really wanted to do was keep writing and recording music. But nowadays, performing live (or maybe, for the very select few, cross-branding) is everything: nobody is going to have a career like Kate Bush's any more, being paid to put out albums in splendid isolation. So, the pressure is to "get out there". But until you get to the point of not having to persuade people to see you, gigging can be pretty miserable – plus in my case, it added a dissonant note to my personal relationships, to the extent that I was always hoping that friends would come to our gigs, which I didn't particularly enjoy myself.

- I'd be a liar if I didn't acknowledge that part of me still wishes we had made it. But equally, I'm so grateful to be in a position where I genuinely love making music once more.

—

SIMON TURNER
CELLO PLAYER, HALLE, BBC PHILHARMONIC, ELBOW, BLOSSOMS

Creativity is good for you! Whether it's baking a cake or writing a song, that desire to make something new that didn't exist before is often the thing that gets us up when we've been slumped listlessly on the sofa with nowhere to go and nothing to do. And creativity has always, it seems, been a part of us, from the earliest cave paintings and bone carvings to now, when people all over the world make music, write stories and create pictures in all conceivable environments, political situations and social settings. Making something that isn't directly useful in our lives might just be what makes us human.

But making a cake is not the same as making a song, of course. We bake because we want a sweet treat, a reward. Maybe it's just for us, maybe we want to treat the others around us too - it's a birthday or a celebration, and we want them to feel special. Or maybe we're guilty about something and the cake's a peace offering. Or a show-off bid to increase our social standing. Even cake turns out to be a bit complicated!

What makes us want to write a song? Is there something that's nagging away at us, that can't be expressed to the people close to us, that we need to get out? Or some snippet of a tune, or a chord change, that is floating around waiting to be given a context? Perhaps this is the purest form of musical self-expression, this creative urge to make something concrete from what is within us. It doesn't matter if it's good or bad, or if nobody ever hears it; it just is something that we've made. It might be a safety-valve for our feelings, it might be a chance to work out what we think, it might be another world in which to lose ourselves, away from the horrors of daily life.

So, the song is written, and a little bit of us is out there in the world now. What does the world think? If others might be critical, we better get in there first: what do we ourselves think? Is our song actually good enough to be passed by our internal critic, or do we suddenly lose belief in this thing we've made, and start thinking we're stupid to have ever thought we could write anything at all? The people close to us are almost honor-bound to tell us it's great, so they won't necessarily help us feel more secure. Let's hope the general public like it, then; but they have a multitude of opinions and, in these days of social media, lots of ways of sharing them! Suddenly, our private moment of personal creation has blossomed into not only a potential source of public adulation, but also of public anxiety.

So maybe our song is a flop. Not many people like it that much, but not that many people hate it either. How can they be so indifferent to us sharing something of ourselves with them?! Do we respond by thinking the world is lacking in taste and discernment, and that our music is just too advanced? Or do we think our internal critic was, after all, right and we are worthless musicians with nothing to offer, and therefore probably bad and worthless people as well? Do we believe a bit of both, depending on the time of day?

So maybe our song is a hit and we get to perform it often. Each time we do, we are a little further away from the emotion that prompted us to create it in the first place. So, are we 'faking it'? Or has something else taken over, that lets us conjure up the appropriate emotions even if we're not feeling it at that precise moment? After all, that's what we must be doing when we cover somebody else's song. Creativity has passed, now we're re-creating! Hopefully we can perform with as much passion and commitment as the first time, of course, but it'll be at a certain distance.

Yet there they are, the audience, with their bright shining eyes! They love the song and they adore us; we have managed to write something that encapsulates our own feelings and simultaneously awakens theirs. What could be better than this amazing communion with complete strangers? Still, when tomorrow morning we've got our rubber gloves on to do the washing up, are we the same powerful performer? Which version of us is the real one?

Often, we perform with others, so how do we persuade them to share our vision, and communicate it to the audience the way we want? Being a control freak may seem to be the answer, but if the musicians we share the stage with feel they have no input themselves, are they going to play with real energy and commitment?

Their contributions could alter and improve the song in ways we couldn't begin to imagine; but if they do, is it still our song? Are we able to relinquish our sense of ownership enough to let changes happen? And what about real collaborative writing, where everybody pitches in? It takes a strong ego to want to put your ideas forward, and an equally strong ego to take your fellow band members telling you they're rubbish, and their idea is better!

So, I believe very strongly that creativity is good for us, but not necessarily in the most direct way. Of course, there is the private moment of creative inspiration, or the solitary teenage retreat to your bedroom with a guitar or a cello to get away from parents, school and a world that you don't understand and doesn't understand you. But after that, music is the process of communication writ large. It's talking to yourself, about whether you're 'good enough', or about what the thoughts and emotions in a song mean to you now it's two years after you wrote it. It's talking to your fellow musicians about those feelings and listening to theirs in a way that lets you absorb the reality of their experiences, so they can be part of your music-making together. And it's about having enough inner strength, passion and self-belief to communicate the truth of your musical vision honestly to a whole room of strangers.

Through music, we get a chance to practice these skills over many years, confront our demons and see ourselves improve. I don't think there can be many better things for our mental health.

—

SIMONE NILES
SINGER, AUTHOR, COACH

So, you want to be a musician? Let's face it, it's not the long hours of practice and effort it takes to learn, develop and hone your skills that makes you decide to start this adventure; you do this by default. It's likely to be a mixture of two things: the desire to express yourself through this particular medium and the hope of making a living doing it. The challenge is that what is typically presented in the music industry, is a glorified and romanticised version of music success. The idea of winning awards and being famous seems to become the end goal for many seeking fulfilment and wanting a career in music. The reality is that very few achieve this outcome.

When the end goal becomes about fulfilment and happiness via musical expression and being able to make a living doing so, it changes the attitude and approach, which ultimately affects a musician's mindset and mental well-being. For this reason, I always suggest that you take a deeper look at your core values around what you truly want to achieve. Core values being those significant truths within you that make YOU. In other words, to use an inside out approach. You will certainly be influenced and sometimes affected by the external stimuli, but when you check in with yourself about what you truly want it can make a huge difference.

When I was young I knew I wanted to be a singer and my idea at age seven had nothing to do with winning awards; in fact, far from it. It had more to do with a creative expression or outlet that felt like a 'must' rather than a 'should'. Like something that no matter what others thought I should do, I knew had to do music. It was only as I grew older and saw what the media and industry projected that I thought that greatness had something to do with being famous (to a certain extent). This thinking eventually changed as I realized that my fulfillment would not be given to me, but instead created by me and so I set about making decisions around what would bring me joy and what I loved doing.

Making a career in music is running a business and making money and being known is an important part of it. However, when fame and money become the only focus or driven outcome it creates a warped version of reality. Instead, when the focus is also on making 'good' music and being excellent in your craft, it becomes easier to be known for your high standards. When you split your focus to include creating a fulfilling life and making an impact through your music, it encourages a more holistic view and approach which often brings about a type of success that has little to do with the stereotypically view of 'making it' in the music industry.

Ask yourself, do I really want to be famous? Is my idea of 'making it' real or healthy? The answers to these questions are neither right or wrong, instead they give you an opportunity to honestly address where you are right now and if you don't like it, you have a choice in making changes that better serve you. I encourage you to balance your focus with your values; what inspired you to become a musician in the first place.

There are many musicians who are popular in their field who are not internationally known and are thriving both financially and creatively. Equally, there are famous musicians who are reaping awards and living an exquisite lifestyle who are fulfilled in their musical career. The common thread in these examples is that their driven outcome is likely based on creating their own fulfilment and connecting with their values, which helps them to stay grounded in their work life, which subsequently leaks into other areas of their life in general to promote balance.

There are also several examples of the opposite, where famous or not, musicians struggle to thrive and find it difficult to cope with the pressures of the music industry, their perceived notion of failure and the impact it has on their general well-being. Shifting this starts with taking responsibility of your emotions, thoughts and behaviours in order to create new ways of dealing with the challenges that are presented throughout your musical journey. The industry can only dictate what happens on the outside, but you ultimately dictate what happens on the inside, meaning how you let it affect you.

What this approach can do is to help empower you to be in control of your own destiny. It gives you the opportunity to find what makes you come alive and do that. It creates a space where you can grow through the challenges by using what serves you and discarding what doesn't. The good news is, you are not alone and there is support available to help you succeed. All you need is the willingness, the know-how and to embrace the ups and downs, as they will come to teach a valuable lesson – how to rise and fall and rise again.

—

STEPHEN J KIRBY
SINGER- SONGWRITER

It "hit" about three years ago. My mind was making me believe I was terminally ill. Every morning as I woke, I truly believed it was my last day, no matter how many times this happened it was as real as the day is long. Although now I feel much better I still suffer from Health Anxiety. With this I struggle with my self - esteem, I have a mental vulnerability that chokes every part of my confidence. I feel paranoid of people around me and feel everyone is talking about me in a negative manor, when writing my music this has been a constant strain, nothing is good enough, even when I truly believe in my song I struggle to let be heard. When it is finally "out there" the members of my band will give feedback (they are not fully aware of my mental health issues) they are great people and I feel the most important thing we need is honest and dear friends in all of this, not to be surrounded by egos or "associates" only in it for the music, it's much more than that, it's a journey an adventure together, I feel I'm blessed with my musical family. I cannot talk to them about my health, but I feel, because of my illness a, vicious circle!) Feedback in which will be constructive, with valid reasons for negativity and backed up with a possible solution, that is very important for me. Despite my soul crushing non-belief in my musical ability when I'm on stage or in the studio I feel I'm home, I feel nothing other than a joy, a jubilance that cannot be quashed, then back to reality, EVERY time with a bang. So much so that I took a year away from music, sold guitars and never even listened to the radio! As the years have passed it has gotten easier, more good days than bad. Not a week goes by that I don't think of stopping music, but something always draws me back. Even in writing this am I feeling that it isn't much if any help to anyone, I hope it is. To conclude I can only tell you what gets me by. In truth I don't really know, my family, (my wonderful three children whom believe in me and my wife whom has always been there even at my lowest she was at her best.) the little self believe that begins to write a new song, the fact I can now believe some of the positive comments I receive when performing, surely not EVERYONE will lie to us! Today is a "low" day so I'm trying my hardest to be as positive as I can, and I think that's the golden rule. Knowing there ARE people out there whom can and will help; sometimes in the strangest of circumstances and in the strangest ways! We are NOT alone in this. My music helps me so much, it's ironic to think it also causes me anxiety but it's something that keeps me ME. I hope at least one part of this makes some sense. The mind can be so destructive, but it creates such greatness.

—

TOBY MARKS
ARTIST, PRODUCER

I was born the youngest of three siblings. My brother, the eldest and three years older than me, had severe learning difficulties and epilepsy and was already becoming hard for my parents to manage. The addition of another baby was too much for them to cope with and two years later my brother went away to live in a residential care home.

This meant that one weekend a month was spent visiting him, a weekend of carsickness on the motorway instead of a weekend of playing with my friends.

By nine years old, I was being 'disruptive' at school and was sent to a new one, an hour's journey from home. The school was much more interesting but, inevitably, few of my new school friends lived near me and I was spending more and more time on my own.

My parents were both very driven with their work, and family time was limited to Sunday lunchtimes and summer holidays, with the odd day out or event in between.

Whilst this portrayal may be a bit exaggerated, for that boy the experience of being left alone to entertain himself became normal. In fact, I even started to be proud of being a 'lone wolf' and not depending on a group. Of course, that didn't mean I was getting what I needed emotionally.

At eleven I changed school and did OK for the first couple of years. But within a couple more years something changed, my school results plummeted, and I began to dread, and then hate, having to go there.

By 16 I had had enough but I felt trapped in a day-to-day life I could no longer bear but equally had no control over. On the last day of the Christmas holidays I tried to kill myself. The attempt failed but it did get attention, perhaps my aim all along. My parents were shocked, they had no idea I was depressed. The only thing they seemed to have noticed was that "I was wearing black more lately" and I had seemed quieter.

I left that school and enrolled in a much more relaxed college where I was treated more as a young adult and generally felt I fitted in. By that time, I had discovered the joys of psychedelics and smoking dope. My life had changed for the better, it seemed to me.

Somehow, I managed to get the grades needed to go to university, a welcome chance to escape from the family home at last. It was a wonderful time of discovery for a while, my mind opening to new and wonderful ideas and stimulation. But, perhaps inevitably, by the end of the first year it was starting to feel too constricting. For as long as I can remember all I had wanted to do with my life was be a musician. Studying philosophy was a time-consuming distraction. So, I dropped out.

I continued to live with my student friends but found myself, once again, spending large amounts of time on my own. I read a lot, and drank, smoked and tripped away the boredom. For a while it seemed cool, living the dream of the aspiring, and struggling, musician. But emotionally I was still not fulfilled, and depression was never far away. From those days onwards, I have lived on a rollercoaster of depression, some good years, a lot of bad ones and a growing sense of inevitability.

Once my career took off and I established myself in my dream job of successful musician/producer, the inevitable pattern emerged once again. I ended up working on solo projects, in a studio on my own, performing alone, on a stage on my own. The contrast between being the centre of attention, loved by thousands of fans at a show, and sitting alone in a silent studio was hard to deal with. I had a loving partner and good friends but still I was spending too much time alone.

At the peak of my career a surprise was waiting. Despite all the 'success' I wasn't happy. I was seeing therapists, trying to understand what was wrong, and one day I got an answer.

I woke up on the day of a rebirthing1 session feeling particularly anxious and unsettled. By the time I got to the appointment I was physically shaking. I dove straight in and before long, boom! A sharp, vivid, emotionally charged and deeply awful memory of being raped by a teacher at school when I was 12.

At last I had an explanation for why things felt so wrong. It was all going to be OK....

No. In hindsight it seems this was a symptom, not a cause (in part, at least). Working through this memory revealed to me just how lonely I had been and how vulnerable that made me. Now I knew I had fear of authority and trust issues to add to my problems. Not good.

Fast forward to me hitting 40. I had achieved my dreams. I was an internationally famous and respected musician/composer/producer. I had travelled the world in business class and tour busses, stayed in 5-star hotels, seen pretty much every country I had dreamt of. I had moved to the beautiful cottage in the country with the recording studio at the end of the garden. I had my own record label, I had achieved everything I set out to do. And I was miserable. Despite the years of therapy, I couldn't find peace.

These days I still spend far too much time in a room on my own, glued to a computer. Occasionally making music but more often dealing with the endless drip of emails and paperwork that seem to be the only thing that ensure that any money ever reaches me. For years I have tried to find a way to change this but here I am again. I've just come out of a long period of depression, I'm coping now, enjoying the burst of energy and creativity that coming off antidepressants allows me. But I know the cycle is far from broken.

I'm trying to collaborate with other musicians more now. It's rewarding, and I love doing it but there is still too much that needs to be done alone. It may be me, but I can't see a way out of this. I know that spending too much time alone edges me towards depression, but I can't find a way to break the habit. Too many years of being independent and self-reliant have left me ill equipped to suddenly become a team player. Take direction from a boss I don't respect? Not going to happen. Turn up to work at times not of my choosing wearing clothes someone else has dictated? No thanks.

The way the music industry is set up perpetuates this. If I have something others can make money from then I become interesting for a while. In the meantime, I am invisible, expected to go away and get on with it.

Just like when I was a kid.

1 Rebirthing is a therapy technique developed in the '60s derived from pranayama yoga. It involves cycles of continuous breathing, which seems to allow us to bypass the usual mental blocks and access supressed subconscious feelings and experiences.

—

WAYNE SHOTTON
MUSICIAN

Without a question of a doubt my first port for call points to the Ego within us all and in particular those of us in society who have an inclination for the arts and music. Those people with artistic sense and those of us who produce a piece of art be it with the oil on canvas, or as in my case a musical instrument.

My point of reference is useful I hope since I can be included for two reasons. I have an ego and secondly play the drums. I will try to be objective in this short essay and form discussion from a musician's view. I can reference some experience playing with other musicians and secondly from observing some musician friends of mine who after playing, song writing, producing, have shown some form of depressive tenure or illness based on their life involved with music.

After many years of playing drums, writing, performing, I believe that my own Ego is there but lessened, flattened due to awareness and probably age.

I believe when you're younger, (but all this discussion can apply to any age), your drive to be an accomplished artist/musician very much links to that of idolisation and for the want of being admired, being famous. I believe it's a very powerful objective.

As a musician I've been there in my head. On certain day's I still go there. This, coupled with some or a lot of talent pushes you along the road. You try to play, to be like your idols and those who have achieved stardom. The 'X Factor' is a good example. It was 'Top of The Pops' for me and 'The Old Grey Whistle Test' for the more educated.

Stardom isn't achieved alone and worthy of further writing... and I will discuss, but for now let's keep to the rhetoric of where Mental Health problems may occur.

Playing in various guises, venues, at home, in front of people, being recorded and listened to. I don't think the real problems, other than frustration, occur much at this stage of exploration and performance. The later stages of what is perceived as failure to achieve the glamour, the adoration and status, seem to be where the problems start to manifest in my opinion.

I am writing from the later stage i.e. from playing for years and after accepting what could be perceived as 'failure'. Its important to understand what is often overlooked, misunderstood, that even if you are a complete genius at what you do, and your audience believes this, the fact is, as a performer of one kind or another, you are going nowhere without massive input from powerful business. This is because you are up against the problem of coverage, i.e. huge turf and reaching large numbers of listeners/observers, the cost of it, and if you are/not the current thing that's wanted on the market. You need massive media coverage and airplay. Without this your genius is only just in front of you and around you, family, friends, the admirers at local venues.

Body fluids, blood and guts.

Discussing on a micro level and from my own experience a lot of Adrenaline and Endorphins kick in at gigs and out of playing music/performing.

According to medical science, too much Adrenaline can cause depression, anxiety, fatigue, and sleep disturbances at gigs I've noticed for myself and other members of the band that there's this sort of 'come down' from the experience, a lowering of excitement. The sort of 'come down' you hear about with excessive drug use i.e. Heroin. This may not be as powerful as strong drugs, I don't know, but it rings similar bells. With constant up and down from playing i.e. starting and finishing gigs, not performing, I think I am making a point. Endorphins, according to translation, are groups of hormones which are secreted within the nervous system and brain which activate the body's opiate receptors causing analgesic effects, euphoric highs. I found personally that it has taken me hours or even days to walk away from the rush of particularly a 'good' gig. What's a good gig? Well. This sometimes hasn't even involved a great audience or people in any large numbers but when it all comes together, and the sound is right, the playing comes with this and you are definitely in a zone comparable to the biggest joy ride of your life.

Being local to Manchester I played with my present band at 'Club Academy'. An excellent venue. Low ceiling and acoustically brilliant. It was a Monday night and as you can guess poor turn out due to the usual. People spending money over the weekend and work commitments in the week. So, hardly anyone there watching, but, all that I mentioned before came together. Great sound and playing. Never forgot it and big impact on my system.

Of course, this works on every level for individual people, so you could eat an ice cream and get the same impact or rush.

I also think for performing musicians its about the moment, that special moment and relationship that you find is interactive and personal. Like the unique find or search for the identity in Photography which is my other passion. It's very difficult to get this relationship and deep-seated thinking in 'producing' something from the heart which performers, musicians alike try to share over to the observer or listener. When I'm taking a photograph say a portrait or in my case over the last few years...musicians, I am not just taking shots from a vernacular perspective i.e. everyday shot from a mobile or snap shooting is the easy way to describe this. When my mind is set on capturing something beautiful, let's say in a face, or the personality which is presenting, I am spending time within myself, sort of mirroring my own sense of what is presented in front of me and then trying to share this result or experience with others. This mutuality once shared and agreed upon as interesting and exciting gives rise to praise and adulation. A good song or performance reaches you deeply and is favourable to be experienced again, something that you personalise deep within. Conversely. There's this sort of misconception with digital cameras that there's no art form, i.e. it's easy to hold down the shutter and wait for the good shot to present itself through numbers. People claim to call themselves photographers, well they are technically but that's not an art form really. That's just working without putting thought to it. Well that can be done and is a useful tool in various forms, but when you are trying to reveal and capture real depth and relationship with your 'subject'... that is truly the art form and digital cameras have various tools rather like an easel to get to this. An example of this is that you can never truly discover the art form of taking great photography until really you understand the relationship between 'aperture' and 'shutter speed' in manual mode. I'm not going into this in now, but auto mode will give you results but not genius. All that said, where are we going with this. I try to capture my subjects sometimes in very difficult conditions and only given minutes to represent my art form.

Point being that similarities start to emerge for musicians. A lot of time is spent studying your craft and a lot of self expression is trying to get out there mostly to relatively inexperienced musicians and listeners of music. To finally connect is a rarity and unfortunately a lot of musicians also are firing away in auto mode and can't understand why they aren't getting the idol status that they crave. An exaggerated example of this can be scene on the outtakes of 'X Factor' where people sing flat notes or are just too over weight for the big advertising magazines. This is because to become famous these days you are a more of a selling point, sort of in the auto mode. I.e. if you have the good all round 'figure' but not much talent you can still be sold to make money in auto. You then become by proxy working in auto i.e. being told what to do etc not being inventive at all relying on large numbers to get the status...the good result out of many tries.

Musicians not in auto mode and having studied their craft i.e. understanding relationships between a major and minor key (aperture/shutter speed) and how this support feeling and depth, still have problems because of what I mentioned before...the difficulties of getting seen and needing, industry to get the platform started.

When this misunderstanding and heavy load, exhaustive measures, hit on each other, a lot of performers and artists buckle in my opinion. I've seen it and experienced it with people I've worked with.

Relationships, talent, dries up and the drop can cause low ego, low mood, and personality changes. Lots of musicians use drugs and alcohol to get back the fix, the rush they once had.

ow I had my own issues in those darker realms, but I would say looking back, not, for the reasons of being a musician who is unsuccessful in terms of not being famous. I have felt depression and low. I grew a beard and stopped looking after myself. I know what the drop-in mood feels like. Looking back at it all and still a musician, still playing, still using a camera, sometimes in auto mode for purpose but in manual mode for discovery and invention, I feel I am one of the lucky ones who is still playing and without question feel successful because I have realised that I am a genuine interested in my craft. I don't go around playing in auto mode just to call myself a musician. I do put real thought to it and practise my art form. It's natural for me. I realise that I get my kicks out of 'performing' and understand the walls that present to stardom.

Interestingly at gigs now I notice that I get down when I'm packing away my gear, or, I've got to carry my drums down the street to my car, or, that I've paid a lot of parking ticket money. I get frustrated when the venue doesn't even offer me some water for playing at their venue when they are taking money off people for beer etc.

To finalise: every one's experience is relative to them and their understanding of performing and creation. To understand the walls that present to stardom and the industry in control is one of awareness and possibly, time. I have felt those low ebbs in the body which effect the mind and your state of health and they are very dark feelings and places you can go to. If you can beat this and come through the other side without scares then you are truly lucky.

The brain is a truly remarkable instrument, and once it is fed, needs constant feeding and watering to keep it alive. When the feeding mechanism is affected, the allotment is dry, disrupted, muscle growth can start to disappear, and every aspect of the body can fall into decline, especially thinking and thought processes, emotion. Similarly, when the music, adulation, dries up and the adrenaline isn't evident any more then you as a performer can fall into decline and disrepair making life hard.

Its only when you start understanding the real sense of achievement in yourself and your art form, and you make this, the important factor, can you truly combat the difficulties associated with the mind and mental health issues relative to being a performer, a, creator. The Ego isn't so much affected. It is more understood.

Hope this makes some sense Rachel using metaphor and such to describe/discuss a truly fascinating area to study. It's good that we both come from a platform of understanding and that by sharing ours and others experiences we can help people to understand this grey area which permits to performers and artists and that in some way we may be of help or influence.

—

DOBS VYE
TV COMPOSER, MUSICIAN, PRODUCER, HALF OF PUBLIC SYMPHONY

Goals evolve! Nowadays I am a composer for TV shows, and my goal is to keep winning work until I can retire. I started by learning the ropes for a few years as a co-manager of dance music acts / DJ's and producers, although my interest as a musician was watching in the studio and editing the records. Although I pursued a career progression into A&R, those promises proved disappointingly flaky. So I spent uncomfortably long unemployed, and finally realised I should make my own luck. If I had won the lottery, I would have built a studio to make music, so that's what I resolved to do! Writing a business plan with the guidance from Portobello Business Trust, I launched my business to make music for commercials in 1999, also with monthly monitoring from a Prince's Trust mentor - both invaluable resources to feel legitimate and supported (financially too). Gradually my luck and intent rolled in the direction of creating music for TV shows, mostly factual and entertainment. It's a hustle from one job to the next, and a rollercoaster for mental health, littered with failure and success of commissions. But I now have systems to generate work, believing that there is work out there to be hunted, by being a proactive detective as an essential part of my daily job. Having been a manager, I maybe have a grounding in business-headedness, where other musicians might be apologetic. I don't like to rely on anyone else to source work, so if I am not finding and winning new work, it is down to me, my responsibility.

My independent band Public Symphony, whose 'Inspire' album is a concept journey, won indie awards, and an 'Album of the year' in The Times. We worked so hard and long to make it, and it was a pride and joy. I thought I could market it without a label investing, and spent a lot on CD pressings and PR and videos and radio plugging to set it all up for a 'commercial' style release. But it was a bottomless pit in terms of energy needed, and when kids came along, I could not bring myself to relentlessly promote or gig. With the emergence of Spotify, I lost the belief that an album could be as profitable a business as my TV work. The message of the album is ultimately very positive, yet I felt that the constant need to promote was an overwhelming drain on me, which was a negative, and it was torture to admit defeat to push it commercially. It's out there online for people to discover.

It is a rollercoaster of ups and downs in my world of pitching to compose for TV shows. I have more faith nowadays that if I keep to my systemic ways, that work and income can be achieved, a belief I pretty much abandoned about records. Music is like water, there is so much of it, while cultural breakthroughs and barriers to entry are what made music recordings an especially valuable industry during the 20th century. The universality of access to creation and access to market means that 'making it' (a lifelong income) is up against the numbers (too many competitors, too much content), while the winners nowadays are the distribution platforms.

Rejection is part and parcel of what I do, though it is my responsibility to discover and supply what would please my clients, which depends on successful communication both ways. I learned a lot of lessons in clear communication via self-discovery courses at Landmark Education, which I found fascinating. Hope is to represent the possibility that my creations are useful. Nowadays I don't let rejection mean anything about me, except that they found music that they prefer, or that there is something I could have improved on in my delivery.

I observe a structure in my working hours, usually around 9am-6pm week-days, and draw the line. I know I'm too much of a hermit, and should collaborate more, and press the flesh; that comfort zone is probably not healthy, let alone sitting still for hours on end. So I need release, and exercise is important. Luckily I can play local tennis 3 or 4 times a week, which gets my steps up, even if not always my spirit, as I'm my worst critic on court!

For me, creating music is easier in a good mood, and good health. I still get anxious and jittery when not earning, and grumpy when I lose pitches or prospective income. Especially when I had new infants emerging. Raising a family (three growing boys) is a higher purpose than making records, and a good distraction from work.Now I have a bit more faith that I can make it to the end of a career, because I have put in the hard work to become more established. I still have doubts and dips, but highs too. It's up and down, but the downs fade with time. I am human, and that's how life comes.

—

ALEXANDER DOUGLAS
ARTISTIC DIRECTOR, ADM PRODUCTIONS & ASSOCIATE OF NHS R&D

The Music Industry is Dangerous.

I write this at the beginning of a new research journey into music and mental health – one that seeks to move beyond nice sequences of statements and into the realm of rigorously structured arguments. I also write with a concern for a more appropriate as well as a more helpful use of language. For some reason, we seem to have societally concluded that it makes sense to say 'mental health' when in fact we mean 'mental illness.' And then, we have the small matter of the importance of the phenomenon of music on its own terms – and the fact that music is more easily experienced than understood means that we know less about it than we think we do.

Context: I write as a BAME professional musician (who has covered a vast musical terrain over the past twenty years) and as a trainee philosopher with evolving research interests in mental health, aesthetics, religion and culture (with both language and music at the heart of all my academic work). It is my wholly subjective and entirely considered opinion that a) music is a quite incredible activity, but b) the music industry, per se, is entirely dangerous. What follows does not purport to be a strict piece of 'academic' writing, but it is certainly going to belie my education and formation to date.

I moved to London from Manchester and playing jazz was more or less at the top of my list of professional ambitions. In the very first working jazz group I was privileged to join, one of the band members suffered from acute mental distress and eventually was not able to play with us anymore. The words 'nervous breakdown' were used.

The 2016 Help Musicians UK survey revealed that around 65% of professional musicians have experienced depression in some form and 71% have experienced anxiety in some form. Now, here's where language inconsistency becomes a problem: the words 'can music make you sick?' assume a very specific semantic freight; if one does not process carefully, one will conclude that it is music itself which has the power to make one sick, as opposed to the 'music industry.' [This requires unpacking, but we cannot do that here and now.] My point is that 'music' and the 'music industry' are NOT synonymous. For many years I have said that music (for me) is the 'right game' but the 'wrong industry.' Music is one of the most wonderful activities in which a person can engage, but around seventy years ago there was a man called Theodor (Adorno) and he had a friend called Max (Horkheimer). Long before the internet and social media, the explosion of the pharmaceutical industry and reality TV, these guys engaged in what seemed to a be (for quite a few people) an unnecessarily bleak and vicious assault on Western civilisation. [Now, before I explain this, let me assure you that the technical stuff that follows really does relate to the music industry – and to mental health.]

One of the things that music is said to do is offer a framework for the expression of one's own individuality. Certain philosophers (Hegel being an especially important example) took it for granted that there is such a thing as universal human desire and that part of this is a (universal) desire to be one's own individual self (however construed). One of the ideas I have taught for many years is that all artists have to decide if they want to 'express themselves' or 'communicate.' One of those requires an 'audience' and one does not. One can technically 'express' on one's own (even if we usually imagine the expression of oneself to a listener) but 'communication' cannot actually take place unless there is at least one other human mind to receive said communication. So, in this sense, 'expression' is nowhere as important to music-making' as 'communication.'

But what does it mean to communicate in music? Why does music itself matter? The famous Harvard evolutionary psychologist/cognitive linguist Steven Pinker notoriously describes music a 'auditory cheesecake' and thus inferior to language (this is in a book entitled How the Mind Works which is much more 'academically' influential that the writings of musician-turned-neuroscientist Daniel Levitin, whose This is Your Brain on Music simply has not had any real 'academic' impact despite selling nicely. Levitin has, unsurprisingly, a rather higher view of music than Pinker but is not read in psychology classrooms around the world in the same way Pinker is). According to Pinker, music merely makes us feel pleasure (like pornography, another example he gives of what he ascribed as a 'pleasure technology') – and one imagines that this applies more or less equally to listening to music as well as making it. Music has no actual functional benefit – unlike language, without which something is lost in the whole experience of being human.

So, we have a super-famous cognitive linguist (Pinker, himself the disciple of the even more famous Noam Chomsky) who is a confirmed atheist who believes in the relative worthlessness of music itself. We also have one of the most famous names in 20th-century philosophy (Adorno), also an atheist who certainly believed in the importance of music itself but had nothing good to say about a Western 'culture industry' (of which music was a vital part, and suffered as a consequence). Adorno would have agreed with Pinker on the worthlessness of much that passes for 'music' in the late 20th and current 21st centuries – but this is where I hope that someone will not miss this: Adorno is usually portrayed as a proto-European dead white male who only valued dead white classical composers and didn't respect jazz at all. As I now own several of Adorno's most important writings and am reading through them very carefully for myself, I see a rather less reductionist-simplistic picture. One need not agree with Adorno's aesthetic preferences to respect his level of argument and his commitment to promoting music as a vital force that requires the best level of thought and commitment of which we are capable. I wish I could say more about this but perhaps you'll read some of my writing on this in more detail elsewhere in the future. Let me try and move this particular plane of thought forward. [And if you're wondering why I mentioned the religious positions of Pinker and Adorno, it is because I am also researching music, religion and mental health and want the readers of this piece of writing to know that when I say that the music industry is dangerous, it is not because I have imposed my personal religious values on a secular industry. It is true that religious people (like me) often make such egregious errors, but I do my level best to avoid those kinds of mistake.]

The darkness of the situation becomes increasingly apparent. There is a difference between 'specialisation' and 'professionalisation' and part of the fabric of the reality of professional music-making is that in being 'commodified,' it is now part of an 'industry' and part of the undergirding ideology of industry is not that there are a thousand items each representing an individual (geno)type for sale to a thousand people; rather, the idea is (still) to sell to a thousand people, but to sell 100 different types of item, or 50, or 20, or 10, or 5, or better yet, just one. We need more sales, but less products, which means higher profits for less people and less ideas/views/perspectives being sold (literally!). If a thousand different artists release their own album and they each sell one, that's a thousand different records that have been sold but a sale of one is not an industry. When one artist sells a thousand records, that's not only a different business reality, that's a different social reality. If ten people decide to buy one artist's record, it is not only that the artist in question has made ten sales to ten different people: if all ten buyers could only afford to purchase just one album, then other artists who may have gotten a sale from some of those buyers will not.

And when livelihoods/reputations/senses of self depend on sales, things are guaranteed to become terribly complicated. While the professionalisation of music is one thing, the ever-evolving challenges involved in making music mean that for an 'industry' to actually exist -much less grow – some voices MUST be sacrificed! Because specialisation would allow us all to make music to whatever standard, but the 'market forces' dictate that not everyone talented and deserving enough to make money from music will succeed in making money from music. And social forces dictate that whatever makes money plays to the market. And so, Adorno and Horkheimer argue that the culture industry is a consequence of a social order which teases people with the prospect of catering to their individuality but in fact, their individuality has already been sacrificed for a collective social order driven by a capitalist agenda much more comprehensive than that envisaged by Marx.

I personally believe that the diseased 'culture industry' of late modernity and post-modernity has contributed to the devaluing of all arts in more places of mind than many of us have realised. Some years ago, I read a feature in a UK newspaper (sadly I forget which one) that had researched the study backgrounds of British and European politicians, and the UK politicians were – on paper – the least artistically/culturally literate across the countries surveyed. Look at what gets airtime and column inches: not a) a lovely jazz duo in a country pub playing heartfelt renditions of enduringly popular (and justifiably so) material from the 'Great American Songbook;' b) a singer-songwriter in a showcase event who no-one has ever heard of but who wows a small crowd with her unique wit, charm, great guitar playing, better singing and even better songs; c) an opera workshop group at an adult education institution that helps so many people find and rediscover their voices; etc. Instead, it is Simon Cowell and his cronies, acolytes, and other fame-hungry types who offer no example (in life or music) worth following but are all the more known for that. If Steven Pinker is culturally limited but thinks that he is intelligent and observant, then on the basis of what he sees exported as 'music' from the 'industry' – music is indeed worthless! So philosophically, one question would be: is the 'music industry' the right place to find excellent examples of 'music?'

We all know the answer to that question: 'sometimes, yes - but often, no." So, if much of what the 'music industry' produces is in fact 'anti-music' – then the music industry is a potentially very difficult place for real musicians – and that is why it is so dangerous.

The music industry really is a more dangerous place than people are able to get their heads around. It offers a tantalising set of prospects for creativity and self-actualisation whereas in fact the parameters are already determined and if one fits into those, the gatekeepers open the doors to a new artist who is determined to 'do what it takes to succeed.' But what is the price of success? And how does one cope when one discovers that the game one thinks one has been playing is not only not being played on a 'level playing field' but there is a set of rules that one has never been told. Professional musicians are indispensable to social life: parties, weddings, funerals, the rest – but even in the 21st century if you marry one you risk impugning your place in the social pecking order.

Now, I'm going to close on a personal note. I personally have struggled with serious mental distress and you know what kept me from becoming a mental health service user?

Being able to play jazz piano really seriously. To be able to think, reflect, question in profoundly metaphysical ways without recourse to language was a massive blessing and while my life and identity is no longer bound up with playing the music, without the music itself I would not be here. That's why I cannot tolerate it when musicians choose to be lazy and slipshod. Music is much, much more than a mere 'language of the emotions' (as Derick Cooke famously argued in 1959 - an argument that was nicely disembowelled by John Blacking fourteen years later). Music requires cognition beyond emotion and can powerfully affect cognition beyond emotion (and I do NOT mean the now widely derided/discredited so-called 'Mozart Effect'). The late great Bill Shankly, a serial winner as manager of Liverpool Football Club once said that football was more important than life and death. He may have had a twinkle in his eye that some chose to ignore, but perhaps the act of making and creating music needs to be restored as an activity that people engage with holistically – and shows such as X-Factor need to be eviscerated into oblivion. Music might be more important to life (and death) than we realise; words can only do so much for mental health and when they run out of steam, we will always have music.

—

ALENA HEREL
SINGER, SONGWRITER, VOCAL COACH

There are so many pressures in life that can impact, affect and alter your mental health. To be honest, I hate the term 'mental health' as the generation that I'm from used the word 'mental' and other words such as 'retard' to describe anyone that was deemed to be 'nuts', insane or challenged. So, to admit to suffering with mental health has always been horrible. Also 'mental health' covers such a broad spectrum (from those who experience 'low days', to those who are bipolar, to those who have multiple personalities and other psychotic disorders etc.) that I believe there should be a group of terms to describe the varying degrees of the battles of the mind including 'emotional health'.

I can only really talk about depression as opposed to mental health at large. Working out how to be human and navigating your way through this thing called life, is hard! So, it's difficult to know whether the music industry creates or just exacerbates the development of depression for some of those who function within it. What I've discovered from my own experience and that of fellow (musician) friends, is that we are definitely more susceptible to feeling 'blue' and to battling with depression and/or other mental health issues.

There are usually varying reasons for this, with the obvious use of drugs probably having a direct impact on the mind, but the common issues that seem to be the main stumbling blocks and triggers within my circles are:

- 1 money/finances; not having a stable, guaranteed income which causes worry and anxiety

- 2 Success/failure; 'making it' but then not being ready for the pressures that come with it. Or not making it or gaining the recognition and/or status that's desired, which is then taken as 'failure'

- 3 Creativity; being open to the external or having a creative mind means that you're more sensitive to emotions, feeling and auras. You have a propensity to experience dark moments (or longer periods) which in themselves can help or propel ideas and creativity, but can also cause bouts of depression, self-doubt and adversely affect confidence and self-belief

If you struggle with yourself as a person - maybe due to childhood experiences or low self-esteem etc. being a 'creative' can definitely trigger certain memories or cause reflection and openness to emotions, thoughts and feelings. Music can sometimes offer an outlet for these feelings - production of songs, compositions etc. but the process of working through them can trigger all kinds of reactions.

Or maybe it's related to personality types. Most of the creatives that I know who suffer with depression seem to be quite confident and outgoing, but in their own space they withdraw and struggle with life. (These are usually the people who compose and create from scratch as opposed to those who read music and perform what's in front of them.)

The fear of sharing your heart can cause immense anxiety. If you're a creator, sharing your work with others can throw up so many different feelings and questions such as - will people like it? Will they like me? Will they think it's good? Will they think I'm good? If they don't like it, is that because I'm rubbish and not good enough? Particularly if you write and perform your own original music/material, there's a lot of emotions and questions attached to your work. If you're not strong mentally, it can wreak havoc with your self-belief and how you view yourself, which can then impact your state of mind/emotional well-being.

•

And I feel that these contributions are a perfect end: the soul of the book. I hope that everything has been rounded up, packaged, presented in a way you can digest and mull over. I hope that you've read about things that have shocked you, that issues are now in your consciousness that weren't there before. If you're in the music industry, I hope you've read some of the stories and found that they have resonated with you, maybe from personal experience or someone you know.

And most of all, I hope, with all my heart that this has provided support for people who need it; the record producers, tour managers, publicists, recording engineers, stage managers, music journalists, A&R- Co-Ordinators, roadies, administrators, managers, vocal coaches, tutors, festival organisers, artist managers, sound technicians, music directors, booking agents, conductors, live DJs, promoters, musicians and many more. That indirectly, the people who are in a position of managing or working with potentially vulnerable people have realized that things need to change, and they need to start being a little more aware of musicians with mental health issues. Together, we can all start talking more, asking how people are doing and really mean it, listening when they're going through a tough time. The music industry is not here to exploit, it exists as a platform for talented musicians to release their music, entertain, be free to express who they are. The music industry is here to support those involved and enable them to work and make a living. It's a wonderful invention, bringing music to the entire world.

"My heart, which is so full to overflowing, has often been solaced and refreshed by music when sick and weary"

— Martin Luther King

Thanks

I would like to thank everyone who contributed to this book. You have made this book possible, you have made it what it is and you have been so open and willing to share and help others that I am humbled by it. Special thanks to Pete Wilson, Heidi Dewhurst, Hak Baker, Louis Barabbas, Toby Marks, Simon Turner, Chris Difford, Karl Walsh, Carol Hodge, Chesney Hawkes and Wayne Shotton.

To all the people who allowed themselves to be interviewed, and who are as passionate about this as I am- thank you.

And an extra thank you for putting up with all my pestering over the past months, you were all so gracious about it.

A huge thank you to all of the musicians who have shaped our music industry, who have been open and honest about their mental health struggles and not afraid to share. And to all the musicians we lost far too soon.

To all of my counselling clients, past, present and future, thank you. The clients who have allowed me to add their experiences to this book, thank you.

Thanks to Catherine Jackson for taking a chance on me and my idea and publishing my first article on music and mental health in Therapy Today in 2017.

Thanks to all the guests I've had on my radio show, you've inspired me to write this and for the direction it took.

To all of the musicians I've met over the past 18 years who's hard work, passion and complete brilliance have made me who I am and kept me doing what I'm doing for so long. Thanks for the encouragement and companionship. Special thanks to Pete, Jason Brown, Sarah Brandwood-Spencer, John Stewart, Sebastian, Alena Herel, Flexie.

The same goes for all of the non- musicians (but music lovers) in my life also who have supported me in my music over the years, throughout my counselling training and all of my musical endeavours, you all know who you are.

And to the incredibly talented and amazing Lindsay Lewis, who, as usual was my go-to for all art work and creative stuff. She has always been a constant support and wonderful friend since 1984!

Anna- thanks for the advice which was a total game-changer for me and the book.

Thanks to Mum, for, well, everything.

And to Chris, Joni and Crosby for being the reason for all things.

Organisations for help and support

SUPPORT FOR MUSICIANS AND MENTAL HEALTH

Help Musicians
24/7 Helpline - 0808 802 8008

Music Support
24/7 Helpline- 0800 030 6789
helpline@musicsupport.org

BAPAM- British Association For Performing Arts Medicine
www.bapam.org.uk
Professional musician advice and support regarding money, legal advice etc
(Helpmusicians also provide support around these issues)

ISM Incorporated Society of Musicians
www.ism.org

Musicians' Union
www.musiciansunion.org.uk

MENTAL HEALTH SUPPORT FOR EVERYONE

Samaritans
UK- 116 123
Ireland- 116 123

Bipolar UK
www.bipolaruk.org.uk
A charity helping people living with manic depression or bipolar disorder.

Whether you're concerned about yourself or a loved one, these helplines can offer expert advice.

Anxiety UK
www.anxietyuk.org.uk
03444 775 774 (Mon-Fri, 9.30am-5.30pm)

Cruse Bereavement Care
www.crusebereavementcare.org.uk
0844 477 9400 (Mon-Fri, 9am-5pm)

CALM
www.thecalmzone.net
CALM is the Campaign Against Living Miserably, for men aged 15-35.

Depression Alliance
www.depressionalliance.org

Men's Health Forum
www.menshealthforum.org.uk

Mental Health Foundation
www.mentalhealth.org.uk

Mind
www.mind.org.uk
0300 123 3393 (Mon-Fri, 9am-6pm)

No Panic
www.nopanic.org.uk
0844 967 4848 (daily, 10am-10pm)

OCD Action
www.ocdaction.org.uk
0845 390 6232 (Mon-Fri, 9.30am-5pm)

OCD UK
www.ocduk.org

PAPYRUS
www.papyrus-uk.org
HOPElineUK 0800 068 4141 (Mon-Fri, 10am-5pm & 7-10pm. Weekends 2-5pm)
Young suicide prevention society.

Rethink Mental Illness
www.rethink.org
0300 5000 927 (Mon-Fri, 9.30am-4pm)
116 123 (free 24-hour helpline)

SANE
www.sane.org.uk/support
SANEline: 0300 304 7000 (daily, 4.30-10.30pm)
Textcare: comfort and care via text message, sent when the person needs it most: http://www.sane.org.uk/textcare
Peer support forum: www.sane.org.uk/supportforum

YoungMinds
www.youngminds.org.uk
Parents' helpline 0808 802 5544 (Mon-Fri, 9.30am-4pm)

WOMEN SUFFERING FROM ABUSE

Refuge
www.refuge.org.uk
0808 2000 247 (24-hour helpline)
Advice on dealing with domestic violence.

Women's Aid
www.nationaldomesticviolencehelpline.org.uk
email: helpline@womensaid.org.uk (you will receive a response within 3 working days)
0808 200 0247 (24 hours)

ADDICTION (DRUGS, ALCOHOL, GAMBLING)

Alcoholics Anonymous
Phone: 0845 769 7555 (24-hour helpline)
Website: www.alcoholics-anonymous.org.uk

Gamblers Anonymous
www.gamblersanonymous.org.uk

Narcotics Anonymous
www.ukna.org
0300 999 1212 (daily until midnight)

EATING DISORDERS

Beat
www.b-eat.co.uk
0808 801 0677 (adults) or 0808 801 0711 (for under-18s)

Anorexia Bulimia Care
www.anorexiabulimiacare.org.uk
03000 11 12 13

RELATIONSHIPS

Relate
www.relate.org.uk
0300 100 1234 (for information on their services)

References

https://www.helpmusicians.org.uk/news/latest-news/can-music-make-you-sick

https://en.wikipedia.org/wiki/Brian_Wilson

https://www.changedirection.org/brian-wilson/

https://www.theguardian.com/music/2015/nov/22/janis-joplin-teenage-traumas-little-girl-blue

https://www.upvenue.com/music-news/blog-headline/1026/the-27-club-musicians-who-died-at-27-years-old.html

https://www.telegraph.co.uk/men/thinking-man/11515605/Kurt-Cobain-was-not-a-tortured-genius-he-had-an-illness.html

https://www.rollingstone.com/music/music-features/the-last-word-stevie-nicks-talks-aging-addiction-fleetwood-macs-future-116754/

https://www.rollingstone.com/music/music-features/the-last-word-stevie-nicks-talks-aging-addiction-fleetwood-macs-future-116754/

https://www.dailymail.co.uk/tvshowbiz/article-2528229/Britney-Spears-opens-suffering-social-anxiety-new-documentary-I-Am-Britney-Jean-megastar.html

https://www.cosmopolitan.com/uk/entertainment/a10221529/britney-spears-mental-health-struggles/

https://www.theguardian.com/music/2015/nov/06/justin-bieber-says-achieving-fame-young-nearly-destroyed-him

https://www.popjustice.com/thenews/siobhan-donaghy-has-been-discussing-sugababes-1-0/

https://www.psychologytoday.com/us/blog/in-the-trenches/201106/the-child-performer

https://www.independent.co.uk/arts-entertainment/music/features/independent-artists-music-industry-stormzy-aj-tracey-stefflon-don-hardy-caprio-major-label-streaming-a8110936.html

https://www.uncut.co.uk/news/bruce-springsteen-reveals-he-s-been-in-therapy-for-30-years-32171

https://en.wikipedia.org/wiki/Elliott_Smith

https://en.wikipedia.org/wiki/Ian_Curtis

https://en.wikipedia.org/wiki/Kurt_Cobain

https://www.telegraph.co.uk/men/thinking-man/11515605/Kurt-Cobain-was-not-a-tortured-genius-he-had-an-illness.html

https://www.thesun.co.uk/tvandshowbiz/4403586/robbie-williams-cancels-his-tour/

https://www.hollywoodreporter.com/thr-esq/read-full-details-keshas-disturbing-740699

https://www.dailymail.co.uk/home/event/article-5554463/Will-Young-perils-fame.html

https://www.theguardian.com/lifeandstyle/2016/jul/01/laura-mvula-i-wouldnt-be-here-today-without-my-brother-and-sisters-love

https://en.wikipedia.org/wiki/Michael_Jackson

https://www.psychologytoday.com/us/blog/mining-the-headlines/201006/michael-jackson-king-pain

https://metro.co.uk/2016/09/18/mel-c-says-life-as-a-spice-girl-caused-depression-eating-disorders-and-obsessive-over-exercising-6135562/

https://www.healthguideinfo.com/anorexia-nervosa/p88411/

https://www.cosmopolitan.com/entertainment/celebs/a13073989/kelly-clarkson-body-image-interview/

https://www.dailymail.co.uk/home/event/article-3187152/Boy-George-reveals-secrets-remarkable-reinvention.html

https://www.independent.co.uk/news/people/profiles/calmer-chameleon-boy-george-on-doing-drugs-doing-time-and-stomping-the-comeback-trail-1938282.html

https://en.wikipedia.org/wiki/Nick_Drake

The Biography Nick Drake: Patrick Humphries, 1998, Bloomsbury Publishing

https://en.wikipedia.org/wiki/Barbra_Streisand

References

https://abcnews.go.com/Entertainment/video/sept-11-1995-barbra-streisand-admits-extreme-stage-46912546

https://www.dailymail.co.uk/news/article-3138134/Abandoned-abused-suicidal-Nina-Simone-s-daughter-52-reveals-abuse-hands-mother-shocking-documentary.html

https://www.dinnerpartydownload.org/liz-garbus-nina-simone/

https://en.wikipedia.org/wiki/Nina_Simone

Straight Outta Compton, 2015

The Defiant Ones, 2017

https://www.bing.com/videos/search?q=2016%2c+lil+wayne+stated-+%e2%80%98%e2%80%99i+have+never+experienced+racism&view=detail&mid=3078F540E6C1189658E03078F540E6C1189658E0&FORM=VIRE

https://www.time-to-change.org.uk/news/black-and-minority-ethnic-communities-faced-double-levels-discrimination

https://eluxemagazine.com/magazine/female-sexualisation-in-pop/

https://www.theguardian.com/science/2015/jan/21/suicide-gender-men-women-mental-health-nick-clegg

https://www.rollingstone.com/music/music-news/read-eddie-vedders-moving-tribute-to-older-brother-chris-cornell-196251/

https://www.eonline.com/news/854032/inside-chris-cornell-s-lifelong-struggle-with-fame-the-soundgarden-frontman-battled-demons-as-he-became-a-rock-god

http://www.chriscornell.com/tribute/chester-bennington/

https://www.bing.com/

https://www.changedirection.org/talinda-bennington-320-changes-direction/

https://www.rcpsych.ac.uk/mental-health/problems-disorders/cannabis

Rachel Jepson has been a singer, songwriter and performer for over 20 years. She is also a qualified counsellor and supervisor. She founded Counselling for Musicians at the start of 2017, working with musicians and their mental health. Rachel has counselled clients from BIMM and The RNCM amongst others, and delivers training on how tutors can help manage students suffering with anxiety and depression. Rachel is frequently asked to speak at music conferences and give talks and training on recognising mental health in the music industry. She hosted her own radio show talking to Musicians about mental health in the music industry, which was a huge inspiration to this book.

Because of the lack of education on mental health issues within the music industry, Rachel developed the first and only CPD accredited course on Mental Health Awareness in the Music Industry. She has been published in Therapy Today, The Unsigned Guide and more.

Due to her own mental health struggles, it is Rachel's hope that everyone in the industry has access to education and support and that this book provides a little bit of that.

Printed in Great Britain
by Amazon

40816838R00119